Praise for *Why Shouldn't We Hire You?*

"In today's hiring marketplace, so many of those who interview for positions absolutely miss the mark because they consider the interview to be a "show and tell" about either themselves or their tasks they've performed at their jobs. What most major corporations seek today is a person who is a good fit for their culture and working environment. Harmony is critical to team success. This book looks at behavioral interviewing and the secrets to presentation that demonstrate to the company that you are not only a fit but that you understand yourself and how to communicate that to others. This book is a first class example of interviewing excellence at its best."
—Fred Coon, LEA, JCTC, CRW
Chairman, CEO Stewart Cooper & Coon, Inc.

"The book, *Why Shouldn't We Hire You?* is an informative and insightful self-help book I wish I had read before interviewing."
—Cheryl McPhillips, Manager of the Constellation Integration Division, NASA, KSC

"As a recent college graduate who recently had to interview for admission to a professional graduate program, I thought while reading the book that it would have been very helpful back when I was interviewing."
—Drew Zolp

"It is an excellent read for anyone who is seeking to strengthen their interviewing and negotiating skills, thus increasing their chances of success in their career path. This book is sure to give a competitive edge to first-time and seasoned job-seekers alike."
—Corinne Hill

"An excellent read . . . I plan to send a copy to all my children and grandchildren for Christmas."
—Karl Richmond,
Chairman, Silver Springs Bottled Water Company

"As a "must read" guide, this book will give its readers — at all ends of the job-seeking spectrum — the ability to stand out positively in any job search interview."
—David H. Lieberthal

"Recruiting firms should require this as mandatory reading for their agents to help them coach perspective candidates."
—Tim Miller

". . . wonderfully detailed guide for successful job searches and career management."
—Nancy Smetanka

"This is truly a great tool in the demanding discipline of job search and employment."
—Paul P. Bazylak, Visa Inc, VP Merchant Relations

"Written in a clear and concise manner, the book is easily read and understood. Tips and techniques abound. Anecdotes and humor interspersed throughout drive points home."
—Alice Nielson

"*Why Shouldn't We Hire You?* does a great job outlining the interview process and gives appropriate guidelines to follow to achieve a successful interview."
—Steve Shepard, PT

"Two very experienced authors provide expert advice and guidance in this book."
—Robert Torres, Director of Public Works, City of Cocoa Beach

"*Why Shouldn't We Hire You?* Is an excellent resource for anyone in the workplace who wants an extra advantage in meeting the challenge of getting hired and staying employed."
—John M. Neis, BBA, MBA, JD

"This is a well written book that would appeal to anyone who is seeking employment."
—Sandy Sutherland, Mortgage Broker

"*Why Shouldn't We Hire You?* is an enjoyable read that all job seekers can benefit from, as well as a good reference book to keep on the shelf during one's entire career."
—Bylle Snyder
Retired Regional VP for Operations, Western Region
Drake, Beam, & Morin (DBM)

"Venckus and Endress have taken us to the leading edge of today's proven interviewing strategies. A must read."
—Michael J. Vandermark, PhD
Founder, International Coaching & Training Institute

"An excellent text for those just entering the job market, or for the thousands wandering in the great unemployment abyss wondering why they can't "close the deal" with prospective employers."
—Bob Glasco
Vice President, RWPC

"The book ought to be required reading for all high school seniors and college students."
—David Dopp
Windcrest, Texas
Retired Mortgage Banking Senior Executive

"Endress and Venckus help prepare you for that critical initial contact by looking at you from the employer's perspective."
—Richard B. Elliott, retired
Regional Director, Asia Pacific,
The Sherwin Williams Company

WHY SHOULDN'T WE HIRE YOU?

How to Create a Successful Interview

David Endress
and
Ron Venckus

The Writers' Café Press, Indiana

WHY SHOULDN'T WE HIRE YOU?
How to Create a Successful Interview

Copyright © 2007 by David Endress and Ronald Venckus

Visit our website at www.whyshouldntwehireyou.com
For bulk purchases of Why Shouldn't We Hire You, contact the
publisher at admin@thewriterscafe.com

Chapter Cartoons drawn by John Bertoncino III
VEEK © John Bertoncino III

Cover Art by Cynthia MacKinnon

A The Writers' Café Press Book
Published by The Writers' Café Press
Lafayette, IN 47905

Endress, David
Why Shouldn't We Hire You?/ David Endress and Ronald Venckus
        p. cm.
        LCCN: 2007928925
        ISBN-13: 978-1-934284-02-5
        ISBN-10: 1-934284-02-5

        1. Employment interviewing I. Title
HF 5549.5.I6 E532007
650.14'4—dc22

Printed in the United States of America

Acknowledgements

FIRST OF ALL, WE want to thank all the clients we have worked with over the years. In total, these individuals represented every organizational level needed in companies. Many came from the Fortune 500 but there were also individuals who were downsized from privately held companies and family businesses. Some had worked years to obtain their position/ role. We have coached thousands of people about their sense of purpose, passion, work fulfillment, skills, competencies, joy, and more often to clear up confusion about the paradigm shifts of career management. The techniques and processes presented in this book are the result of coaching those individuals to new levels of understanding about themselves and reaching employment decisions.

Many clients have shared that learning to be comfortable during an interview has also led to better social/ personal awareness. Specifically, once they acquired an understanding of personal competencies/ behavioral traits, many felt better equipped to communicate their thoughts and engage in business conversations, social meetings, as well as, interact with their families. Working with these people and observing their successes was the impetus for this book project.

We would like to single out some people for their contributions. Kathi Vanyo, career transition consultant and former Managing Director, Drake, Beam, & Morin (DBM) Phoenix, provided us with valuable feedback, insight and encouragement. Deep gratitude is owed to Mike Vandermark, psychologist, professor and president of Vandermark & Associates, Inc., a consulting and training firm for organization effectiveness. The authorship path is one thing, but bringing workable thoughts to reality is another and Mike's creativity and insights were a source of encouragement. It has been said that you can lead a person to business but you cannot make them think. However, Frank Rogers Wittie, Psychologist at HP, made us "Think about Thinking" and this resulted in the presentation of many effective and useful thoughts in this book.

Of course the many clients we've had over the years have made contributions. We worked with a wide variety of personalities, needs, emotions, desires, attitudes—some for just a few hours and others for a year or more. We learned from each client and transferred our experiences to other clients—things like sensitivity, consideration, individualizing programs, learning to avoid blind roads, and more. Each success is built upon all that came before and thus demonstrates to us that the ideas contained in this book are real . . . and guess what? *They work!*

Lastly, we would also like to acknowledge our cartoonist, John Bertoncino III.

David Endress

Ron Venckus

About The Authors

A VERY GRATIFYING REALIZATION took place for Ron and David as they worked together to complete this book. Just as they had to be personally committed as Career Coaches/ Consultants to their individual clients, they realized that authoring this project also meant a personal commitment—to their new audience, you the reader. They wanted to make sure that this book provided more than a how-to textbook of answers—David and Ron teamed up, and with their considerable skills and experiences they have created a valuable thought-provoking resource to guide individuals in their job search. The information in this book will help you prepare to deal with the continuous change of today's workplace and in the future. The techniques presented will help you to be better prepared in your jobs/ careers—to decide what you want, where you fit in, and to help you get what you want.

In this team, both authors play a valuable role. Ron is the *Interview Artist*; his design of questioning is like brush strokes on a canvas. He creates original art for the clients to practice. David is the *Out-of-the-Box Thinker*; he develops creative approaches for presenting client accomplishments, as well as, designing re-employment plans with clients. Ron paints the picture and David frames it.

David is looking at his own career transition. He is recognized as an accomplished career consultant with a track record of over thirty years of significant business experience with Fortune 500 organizations. This business knowledge coupled with his broad industry consulting experiences includes development and presentations of organizational change planning and management-career assessment programs. In addition to his recognized consulting activity, David has been an instructor of Organizational Change at the University of Hartford. He has authored studies on: job shifts in organizations, pre-employment testing, implementing company personnel polices and procedures, career transition manuals, and interview training. David's broad 30 years of coaching and direct hands-on experiences brings a real *Walk the Talk* consulting knowledge that is practical and to the point.

David is well acquainted with career management dynamics and the need for continued organizational efficiencies because of competition or costs associated with market change. David has consulted with individuals on personalized career coaching and delivered career decision-making interventions to the Fortune 500. His professional profile includes a track record of proven leadership skills in building effective cross-disciplinary teams, identifying unseen problems, and generating innovative solutions. David has been the recipient of corporate awards for his contributions and support of corporate goals.

David earned his B.S./B.A. (Business Administration) degree from Youngstown State University and served as an Officer in the U.S. Army. He has continued his education in Human Resource Management and Career Decision Coaching at Princeton University and Pennsylvania State University. A frequent speaker and lecturer, guest speaker on FOX 10 TV, contributor to newspaper career articles, David has also hosted a drive-time call-in radio program for a Boston radio show. He is active in professional societies that benefit Human Resource Planning and Career Management. David is a father to a son, Jonathan and a daughter, Amy.

Ron has semi-retired from his role as a Career Consultant but still provides senior executive interview coaching at Stewart Cooper & Coon, a career transition firm in Phoenix, AZ. He has moved into some serious golf coupled with the new challenges presented by semi-retirement. He spent his earlier years growing-up and managing a farm. If you ask Ron about his career he usually will say, *There's nothing special to discuss, I had a good career and I am an average guy.* Ron has spent most of his corporate career employed in some degree of senior Human Resource management roles. His early corporate years were spent in management of functions that directly served the customer. His HR talents were quickly recognized and he moved into major employment functions for companies.

Ron was recruited into the banking industry and was responsible for managing the HR functions at the Director level. As the banking industry experienced major changes, Ron was able to move with the tide of change and propel his career endeavors to include responsibilities for employee environments. He managed HR through several mergers and as many of us have experienced, got caught in the downsizing arena. He spent seventeen years at Drake, Beam & Morin, a company that delivered products and services dealing with the career transition of displaced employees.

Ron is a graduate of Michigan State University (Human Resources and minor in Psychology). He earned a certificate (financial Management, Commercial Banking) from the Pacific Coast Executive Banking School at the University of Washington and is a Veteran of the US Air Force. Ron divides his time between his wife Jacqueline and family, traveling, fly fishing and his love of golf. Ron has three children: Ron, Jr., golf superintendent; Paul, director of golf, and Vivian, hair stylist, and three stepsons: Jeff, John and Jim.

Introduction

Emotional Strength
—You have the capacity to choose what you think about.
If you choose to think about past hurts, you will continue
to feel bad. While it's true you can't change the effect
past influences had on you once, you can change
the effect they have on you now.
Gary Mckay, Ph.D.

- Remove uncertainty and stress from the interview
- Learn how to effectively place key job strengths and behaviors into the interview and get more offers
- Know how to respond to: "So tell me about yourself"
- Identify what is important when building presentations to distinguish yourself and show value in hiring you
- Discover and establish how to build rapport with key executive contacts

THE INTERVIEW PROCESS, THE techniques and concepts discussed in this book are equally effective for the first time job seeker, recent college graduate, and executive-level individual. These techniques and methods greatly enhance the chances of securing the job—faster and more aligned to individual's goals. The interview concepts we provide will not go out of style, whether in job search or career management.

Interview principles have not changed in the collective thirty-nine years Ron and I have been in Career Management although resume styles, letters, e-mails, Internet, and networking techniques may take on different aspects. The importance of interviews has certainly not changed.

While specific questions relating to technical/ application information are different, the behaviors required have remained relatively consistent. The techniques discussed will continue to serve the job-seeker well into the future. Recent articles indicate this is especially important for the *baby boomers*. The survey feedback from this group indicates that a high percentage are not wanting to retire but may pursue different career paths or secure positions that are less demanding.

You may be attracted to this book for many reasons:

- perhaps you are not getting the results you want from the interview process;
- you might want to learn more about the interview process; or,
- possibly you think or know you are not one of those naturals who seem to walk right into an interview and perform.

After many years of coaching individuals in job search processes, we have come to believe that winning interviews doesn't come naturally—it is the result of concrete, learnable techniques and systematic practice.

Whatever your individual situation is, if it involves securing a new opportunity, it will most likely involve one or more interviews. There is a good chance that you will be subjected to interviewing with several people (maybe several interview trips), each having a set of expectations for a successful performance.

In today's highly competitive career marketplace, regardless if you are applying for an internal position or you are a candidate from the outside, be assured that your interviews will contain challenging and quantifiable questions. These interview questions will require examples of your past, present and future potential contributions, accomplishments and behaviors.

For interviewing purposes it's necessary to know what behaviors and accomplishments you bring to the party. The professional interviewer or company executive knows that past performance is usually the best indicator of future performance. By asking behavior-based questions they get a better idea of how well the candidate will do in the position, company, and as a team member.

In today's competitive employment market, success is usually dependent upon a person's ability to understand several factors:

- fit within a company,
- a fair compensation for skills,
- and behaviors that produce results.

Once you have this understanding then it is all packaged into a presentation that demonstrates a can-do (past), will-do (future), and functional fit. So regardless of your qualifications for a position, if you cannot give a winning performance in the interview, you will probably not get the job.

Acquiring effective interview skills can be both exciting and rewarding. It goes without saying that deep down, all of us like to learn about other people as well as ourselves and we want to know how we fit within the world of work. Interviewing is a continuous learning process, like a living resume.

The Human Resources (HR) department is usually responsible for the type of questioning utilized by the hiring authority, as well as the collection of information from the interviews. In the past decade, there were times when the human resources department was avoided; hiring managers wanted to control the employment process. Today the reverse trend is developing; companies need total control of labor costs and consistency in hiring standards. As the applicant you must be prepared to answer the questions with detailed and thought-out answers relating to:

- specific examples of the work you have previously performed;
- the results you obtained; and,
- the differences you made in the management and/ or impact of that position.

The most commonly used interview selection process today is founded upon behavioral-based questions, but there are companies who use informational, situational and traditional interviews, to name a few of the most popular.

We have organized *Why Shouldn't We Hire You?* into three sections: the first section reflects the steps that occur in today's interview stages. The second section: Coaches Corner, is a continuation that provides indepth discussion and further examples on select concepts. The final section is an appendix of additional information and resources.

The exercises are presented in practical useful steps — ready to use and assist with your preparation. Even if you don't score perfectly at first, and are not offered the job, this book will help you to build upon the experience. It will spur your thought-processes and self-reflection, and help to develop the abilities to become an accomplished interviewer. You will be in control to acquire the job you really want.

Study the *Table of Contents*—you will like what you read, and find the information in this book to be very beneficial. So what are you waiting for? Let's get started!

TABLE OF CONTENTS

PART TWO: COACHES CORNER

Veek © 2007

Chapter 1

What lies behind us and
what lies before us are tiny matters,
compared to what lies within us.
Ralph Waldo Emerson

The Art and Science of Interviewing

IF YOU ASK ANYONE who has ever had to look for a job, the majority of people would agree that, like public speaking, the job interview is capable of creating a significant amount of anxiety. Much of this anxiety is due to misunderstandings and misconceptions about the interview process. The reality is that everyone has to participate in a interview to get hired.

Our experiences show that people spend a lot of time memorizing questions (a poor strategy) that may be asked and not enough time preparing a broader examination about who they are. By identifying and then talking about personal behaviors, a person can develop their likeability factor. Often the outcome of interviewing is that the person with more job knowledge doesn't always get the position! The successful candidate is usually the person who can interview well—this is the person who is able to speak confidently about their behaviors and job knowledge. We feel that anyone can be better prepared for the interview process if they:

- know how to present their job accomplishments;
- know how to present their personal behaviors; and,
- have done some good solid corporate research.

You may be wondering about the connection between Art—Science, and Interviewing. It is actually a simple concept that describes the blend of creativity and knowledge, coupled with the right tools, that makes for successful interviewing. When writing this book, it wasn't our intention to create a "how-to" on interviewing. We wanted to provide you with enough solid and thought-provoking information to facilitate your learning on the subject. We want you to learn and discover—ask questions of and about yourself, others and business entities.

Art refers to the creative side of interviewing—learning how to present yourself in terms of job knowledge and skills, personal competencies/ behaviors. The Science part of the equation is the organization of knowledge and the tools you use to gain that knowledge. You need to learn about your: goals, behaviors/ competencies, job knowledge, as well as, how you affect people. The other equally important piece of Science is knowledge about the potential job situation. When you have discovered and have all this packaged up, you will be ready for successful interviewing and be able to answer the questions: Why Should/ Shouldn't We Hire You? Thus, the Art is learning how to present yourself in a masterful way and the Science is gaining and utilizing knowledge.

The employment interview (or series of interviews) you will experience is a mutual exploration. Your potential employer wants to discover if there is a good fit between what you want compared with what the company needs.

A *good fit* is an effective display of:
past *can-do(s)*, future *will-do(s)*, *cultural fit*,
and *behaviors*.

The interview is also a sequence of conversations in which you have the opportunity to learn about the position, company values, and business issues for which you will be responsible and accountable. An important goal is to interview with, and meet enough employees who work for your potential employer. The objective is to gain an understanding of the company's culture and to discover its fit to you. This is especially important when you have spent a considerable tenure with your previous company—if you are not comfortable with the culture, it will weigh heavily on your ability to transition to the new position. The company, on the other hand, can gain several insights:

- the benefits or specific skill set you bring;
- how fast they feel you can transition; and
- whether you would fit into their (team) culture.

The Importance of The Interview

Interviews involve the culmination of all the work that has gone on before. To get the message across successfully, the interviewee needs to take a role, as well as responsibility, for the outcome. Normally, the interviewer will take the lead. As the interview progresses and it seems the questions are not what you expected, you might begin answering or expanding your answers differently. Be poised and professional, but don't be afraid to be assertive in providing answers that will support your candidacy.

Sometimes the interviewer may be inexperienced and the best comeback is to say, *Maybe if I gave you a brief overview of my background and experience it would be beneficial to you. I am very interested in the position, feel I would fit your team, and would like to demonstrate how I might benefit the company.*

It's just as important to have good listening skills as well-timed answers. If you try to take charge and total control of the process you might not convey the information the interviewer requires to reach a decision. The interview is also a demonstration of how you operate and think. The interviewer could conclude that you don't gather enough information before making a decision. The objective for **both parties** is to gain information for further decision-making.

Building Rapport

As an interviewee you are faced with the challenge of answering questions in the strongest way possible in order to influence the person(s) across the table—so they make a decision in favor of you. In addition, the interviewer, if asked, will respond that most of the time the likeability factor helps them favor you. The ability to develop rapport and trust will be as important as job knowledge, track record and accomplishments. Some points about good rapport are:

- have good eye contact and releases;
- smile as the opportunity presents itself;
- sit comfortably in the chair;
- appear alert, attentive, interested and animated (bright-eyed and bushy-tailed!); and
- be careful of mannerisms (ahems, ahs, looking around, fidgeting . . .).

If the interviewer has a display of his hobby in the office make a passing recognition statement; you could also set rapport with a statement about the building architecture or things you have learned in research of the company. The main point is that the interviewer has the opportunity to develop a solid comfort level with you.

The majority of unsuccessful interviews can be traced to a lack of preparation, not a lack of qualifications. Usually if you have passed the prescreening steps and the employer invites you for an interview, she is convinced that you are a qualified candidate. Discussions should be focused on the future, using the past to demonstrate your abilities and interest, while the employer adapts to your potential contributions that will benefit the company.

While making preparations for the interview your success will be based on the following factors:
- the degree to which you demonstrate your knowledge of the company's business issues and how you can positively impact those issues;
- the degree to which you demonstrate your compatibility with future colleagues;
- the degree to which you differentiate yourself from other qualified candidates.

How to achieve success with these factors? This is where your competencies and behaviors come into play.

On certain occasions as we were working with clients, they would bring a particular job, found in an ad or from a referral of sorts, into the counseling session. They would declare that their background was an exact fit for this position. This usually happened a lot in the early stages of the transition to locate a new position. We could be mistaken but we have never seen one of these exact fits result in an offer. Why? The clients thought exact job knowledge was enough—they did not do research about how to present themselves well and often forgot to sell their accomplishments! It was as if their whole mind-set shut down and they expected the new company to see the perfect fit and make them an offer. Never assume anything in the interview process.

Remember, even though the long-range goal is to get the job offer, your immediate objective is to get to the next interview(s). Success is based on convincing hiring authorities that you are the answer to their needs. This can be accomplished by presenting vignettes (past accomplishments) that demonstrate your job knowledge and behaviors, and how these will benefit or address their types of problems.

Dealing with Unusual Interview Situations

At the beginning of this chapter, we mentioned that memorizing potential questions was an ineffective interview preparation strategy—you need to be prepared for the unpredictable! A person must be prepared in order to deal with unusual interview situations with confidence. Below are a few unusual situations and possible strategies for dealing with them.

> a.   The interviewer hogs all the interview time by talking about himself and his position.

Pay him a compliment as to his position and state that you look forward to the opportunity to benefit from his experiences. Then, look for a natural entry point and say: *Based on what you have just shared about your background, I am beginning to understand how my experience* (etc.) *would be very beneficial to your organization. Let me tell you about* ___. Here a short background overview would be useful.

Another approach can be used, if you are comfortable doing it: let him continue to talk—you listen carefully and comment or ask clarifying questions along the way. As a result, he will describe you as a great candidate and good listener.

> b.   The person you are meeting with takes phone calls that are taking up a lot of the interview time.

There are two possibilities for dealing with this situation. You could suggest that you are willing to come back at the end of the day to meet with her so there would be fewer interruptions. You can see she is very busy and you want to have time to learn about the opportunity as well as present your background. *However*, the point of all the preparation was to get this interview—and you may risk the opportunity by suggesting a different time.

The other response is probably more productive: play the patient game, fill in when you can and let the interviewer control the next moves, with some input from you.

> c.   For some reason you sense you are being interviewed for a different job than you are prepared to discuss.

In this situation, the ability to make a quick judgment call and ask for clarity is important. It could turn out the position has more responsibility! Ask the interviewer to tell you more— provide further information on this different position.

First Impressions

Throughout this book, these keys points will be repeated:

- make sure you are on time;
- if the schedule gets changed or there is something going on, wait patiently;
- don't wait for the morning of the interview to have your clothes ready; be presentable;
- sometimes being nervous can lead to chattiness and potential conflict in the waiting area! Instead, be friendly to all you meet, try to learn more about the company, and be constructive in your thinking and comments;
- use a positive mental attitude and never bad-mouth your previous company; this is a good time to avoid any sensitive issues;
- don't show or create a different picture of the real you! You never know who you are talking with and the impact he might have on the interview process;
- answer clearly; if nervous, take a couple of discrete deep breaths;
- always sit in a comfortable natural position in the chair provided. Sit up straight, feet on the floor and stay that way;
- starting with the greeting in the lobby, keep eye contact, but don't stare. Every so often break eye-contact and then re-establish it intermittently— this is something to practice beforehand;
- have your questions ready to ask. If they have been covered say: *most of the questions I prepared*

have been answered . . . then, based on your research, mention several to show you were prepared;

- at the end, always ask what happens next and when you can be expected to return? E.g. What is the next step in your hiring process?

- practice your handshake as if you were running for public office. Give a firm handshake as you leave, thank her for her time and say you are very interested in the opportunity.

Interviews for most folks are unsettling and make them anxious. Your goal is to proceed without omitting any small detail or making a mistake. Often interviewers focus on small details—they have learned that attention to detail on the little things means you will do the big things well.

The Art and Science of Interviewing

Questions to Ask Yourself

- How is presentation an ART form?
- How does preparation qualify as a SCIENCE?
- How can I create a first impression that will leave them wanting more

I see you have not yet completed a career
exam—we must schedule one immediately!

Chapter 2

How often, even before we began-have we declared a task "impossible"?
And how often have we construed a picture of ourselves as being inadequate?
. . . a great deal depends upon the thought patterns we choose and on the
persistence with which we affirm them.
Piero Ferrucci

Career Examination

THE KEY TO SUCCESS is to understand the importance of
effectively managing your own career—know your strengths
and who you are, and recognize your ideal work environment. Unfortunately, most working individuals are so busy
just doing their job, they aren't inclined to take the time to
examine themselves:

- who they really are;

- what behaviors motivate them;
- what talents they employ;
- to which environment they are most suited; and
- what they use to get the work done.

It is important that people spend time in self-reflection—determine what job knowledge and behaviors they possess that result in a job well done. A career examination is two-fold: personal analysis and work environment analysis.

This examination does more than provide self-knowledge and focus to make viable career choices; it will also lay the groundwork for effective presentations to both potential and current employers.

Personal Analysis

Interviewers are interested in your career history. Of course, the chronology of your prior work history is important; it is, however, accomplishments in previous jobs and your behaviors which hold the greatest interest for these folks. A serious career analysis will provide you with knowledge about yourself, open your eyes to viable options, and increase your confidence when approaching a new situation.

To begin your plan, examine your career to date; also examine every aspect of your life. If you look back and reflect, there are several general questions you should ask yourself:

- What do I do best and why?
- What do I like to do and why?
- What kinds of work assignments have I excelled at and why?
- What kinds of assignments have I not excelled at and why?
- Given my responsibilities, how have I made a difference for the company(s) or the organization?

Closer analysis of these areas will reinforce career options as well as lay the groundwork for a strong presentation (whether resume or interview) to a new employer. Think back to assignments that you excelled at and identify your accomplishments. Another source of information is performance reviews received from past managers. There must be certain job skills and competencies/ behaviors that really stand out— you will probably see a pattern develop. At this point, select the top four or five accomplishments that illustrate these strengths; you want to be able to showcase them by having several examples of where and how your strengths have been used in your work.

SARB

To showcase your selected accomplishments, we recommend using the SARB format to help you prepare to discuss your skills and strengths in an organized and effective manner. The SARB formula:

- what was the work: **Situation**;
- what **Action** did I take to solve or prevent the problem;
- what were the **Results** obtained; and
- what **Behaviors** were used (the behavior statement).

Use the SARB structure to effectively communicate successes. For example, in an interview I want to highlight my ability to identify and solve problems. I think of a time when I did this and then apply SARB:

Situation: I saw that we had a problem at the front counter. Waiting clients want an overview of the company and when they approach the front counter, the staff is often too busy to provide a full description—information may be omitted or even inaccurate;

Action: I did some research and discovered that some organizations provide their frontline staff with information booklets to pass out. I designed a model booklet and then presented my findings and model to the management;

Result: The booklet was printed in large quantity and distributed to the front counter as well as other areas that dealt with clients. Today clients are provided with accurate information in a timely fashion and we have increased our clientele by 25%;

Behavior: This example demonstrates my positive approach to identifying and solving problems by using my strengths in research, making presentations. It also demonstrates my attention to ensuring client satisfaction.

To provide supporting evidence for your skills and strengths, you should assemble an inventory of at least twenty vignettes. So, for each job requirement, you will be ready to provide examples (accomplishments) for support.

Pick and choose which vignette(s) is most appropriate in each situation. For example, on a resume choose the most significant accomplishment, as a resume has a 'time frame.' However, an interview situation can be totally different. First of all, there is more time for presentation, and secondly, be prepared for all eventualities—your portfolio of vignettes can act as a contingency plan.

A personal analysis will facilitate good organization when presenting yourself to an employer and it will also help effectively explain how your skills and personal behaviors could aid the organization.

Complete awareness of yourself will include areas in which you were not as successful. The SARB structure can be applied here as well and this knowledge will be valuable in several ways, for instance, to pinpoint areas to work on—whether job knowledge or behaviors—so you can take action to improve. As well, in an interview situation you will probably be asked about weaknesses or areas that need improvement—this analysis will prepare you with a ready answer (of course, be selective about what you choose and be able to provide information about steps you are taking/ have taken to remedy this area).

A thorough analysis of your strengths and areas of need may confirm what you already know about yourself, but it could also bring some surprises. The important thing is that you gain a thorough self-knowledge in order to make informed decisions about your career. The knowledge that you have accumulated needs to be applied to the second step in a career examination—determining your ideal work environment.

Identifying My Ideal Work Environment

How do we discover the why of our actions involving job knowledge? Well it takes time to sit quietly and discover what you actually do during a particular day. As you precisely define your assets, you will be able to consider your market and what the employers may need in specific background.

Example: Today my first task was to begin preparation for a management meeting.

- What was my first thought? – Why was it my first thought?
- What was I thinking about to get the desired result?
- Why did I want to present certain information and leave out other data? – Did this have anything to do with how it would make me appear in management's observation?

If we could assess each of our days in this fashion, just think how much discovery we would make about our personal behaviors.

Let's answer the question, *What Are You Really Like*—as a person, as a thinker, as a partner, as a friend. Often too many of us are on good behavior and dismiss all the rough edges from our minds—therefore in communications we present information that does not really reflect our true selves. The rough edges are still there but they are recessed to our internal thoughts. It is the same roadmap with the interview, not enough in-depth information is transferred. This leads to having most decisions made on limited information. It's more than a matter of knowing what makes us tick or projecting our behaviors from a personal point of view.

The Right Information – A True Story

Assure the *right* information is transferred so a good hiring decision can be exercised and an informed acceptance decision can be made.

Let's begin with considerable thought given to your formative years. Begin by asking those who know you better than yourself. Typically these people are your family, friends, peers, and even some of those folks with whom you didn't have a most favorable relationship.

Here is a good place to mention a behavior that sometimes occurs: when we were working with clients who were recently severed from a company, many of them would say, *Boy I haven't heard from a lot of my friends that I thought would be calling me*. Or it would be the reverse action: I had to tell some of my friends to slow down calling people for me. In both situations it does settle down and people do return your phone calls. They'll get used to the idea you don't have a disease of sorts just because you lost your job and have to transition!

As you continue your career analysis you can re-visit prior performance appraisals. There are assessment tools that you may have participated in such as: a 360 instrument with predetermined questions to be answered regarding the performance of your job. This feedback then is compiled into a report that rates your behaviors (from your supervisors, peers and subordinates).

In some cases you may have had an Industrial Physiologist administer a profile instrument to determine specific behaviors, capability, personality and style. Again the best evaluations are performance/ behavioral oriented.

Don't forget your own input about what happened to you during your formative years. Dr. Mike Vandermark states:

"The *nature versus nurture* argument has drawn considerable attention by psychologists over the decades. On one hand, one can argue human behavior is the product of our environment (parents, educators, living conditions, and so on).

"The opposing view is that we are born with certain characteristics that are hereditary. Presently, the question of whether we are primarily nurtured by our environment or whether nature influences our development more strongly has led to an agreement among many researchers that *both* nature and nurture influence our development.

"So to say 'I am who I am because of my parents (genetics)' is only partially correct. Just as it is only partially correct to say 'I am who I am because of my environment growing up.' It's both. As adults, we are the product of our genetic makeup (nature) and the environments of our lifetime (nurture)."

The following is an analysis of Ron's work history and behavioral development:

In my early years when I would get tired of hearing
my Mother tell me what to do or what I hadn't done,
I would get my fishing rod, call my dogs and head
for the lake so I could be in my own world.

Translation: I have a tendency to walk away from turmoil rather than stay in the fight. This also affected development of good listening ability, negotiating, problem solving and certainly impacted my communication skills.

Since I had to balance running a farm, schoolwork, and a very small social life, I became very dependent on myself to such an extreme that as my career began to develop there was never a doubt that I wouldn't do what I committed to. It was the grass roots of building an independent behavior that is still very strong today. I acquired the desire to please (care giver), perform quality work; I also had a sense of self-awareness. This whole set of factors served me well when I left the farm to military service, and then during my corporate life.

Growing up the way I did and having more responsibility than those I was associating with put me in a position where I wasn't able to develop a healthy empathy level. Showing emotions was a weakness. I could be a member of a team (working group) but I still did my own thing. This required a lot of energy later in the developing years so I had to spend time learning basic relationship management, and business/social skills such as listening, sharing feelings and having patience with others.

Through this example I hope you can begin to see the pictures we can draw about ourselves by revisiting our formative years. These pictures will help us demonstrate who we really are and what environment best suits our behaviors.

So now we look at our school years in terms of what shaped our lives. What subjects did we do our best in and not so well in, and what does this tell us? Don't forget the teachers who helped us to do our work, who we admired, and why. The same idea is used in looking back at our college years or other types of advanced education study. Did we go to the military before college and what form of education did the military provide for us?

Graduation and time to look for our first job. How did you go about getting ready for that important process? What experiences do you recall—which were successful and which were not?

Ron said: My first job offer occurred in a high-pressure situation. As I was responding to an interviewer's questions, he asked me what I knew about making references. My knowledge was some vague information I read somewhere. So, he said that he wanted me to make a reference call. He handed me the phone and a resume. So with no guidance and with him watching, I made the call. Somehow, someway the right questions (logic is a strength for me along with quick mental process and reasoning) were asked. I learned quickly about strengths for me:

- working under pressure,
- dealing with ambiguity,
- working with minimal information,
- using logic, and
- quick processing and reasoning.

Upon further reflection, I realized that many of these behaviors were developed early in life on the farm. These behaviors that I discovered early in my life have stayed with me. They have required continued refinement and development. This is a perfect selling point of a behavior gained early in my life but being used today in an executive capacity.

The latest guides for resumes and presenting your background indicate a focus on the last ten years of your work history. This can be misleading in that, if you only focus on the last ten years for information regarding behaviors, you are short-changing yourself. This guidance or advice is a good ploy to keep resumes short and often leads to an individual not fully exploring personal behaviors gained, developed, and used throughout life.

Simply by starting with the beginning learning years gives knowledge and comfort about who we are and why we got to where we are today. This approach helps provide an understanding as to who and what we are. It builds clarity in the interview and helps determine your goals.

There are and will continue to be different tactics and techniques developed that you can use to get to the decision maker. Once you have completed a behavior analysis and drawn a preference for the type of work you want to pursue, you can prepare your marketing materials.

The focus of writing this book was based on the fact that our clients were not prepared for interviewing because they could not answer these basic questions:

- Who am I?

- How do I manage my career goals? and

- How can I help the organization continually reach its goals?

Work Environment Analysis

In the world of work as we progress up the job ladder we are building career history. It should begin to become clearer that, to excel in an interview situation, you need to know the needs and requirements of the position. This includes published information about the company such as their mission statement, and challenges of the organization as related to the position you are interested in.

As you review your refined portfolio of key strengths, identify where you want to apply these strengths. Research various industries and companies so that you can tie your strengths to the needs and purposes of the organization(s).

Look at the industry that can benefit from your set of skills and has a demand for what you want to do. As you target specific companies for available opportunities there will be published and hidden positions available. If you are using the Internet, you may find published positions that are also appealing.

When you begin developing intelligence about these targeted companies, factor these considerations into the plan:

- geography
- culture
- employees
- organization
- industry type
- size

Start working with your network of contacts to determine if they have information about the companies in which you are interested.

Once you have developed a preferred list of target companies, delve deeper. In order to find the most useful information about a company, your investigation must be focused— set some criteria for research.

Knowledge of the company's products/ services, profitability, customers, growth plans enables you to present qualifications that are specific to the company's needs and show that you are a good fit.

As you gather the data on the targeted companies you may learn of some problems the company is experiencing. This information is invaluable—it will provide you with the opportunity to explain how your experiences and skill set could aid the organization's effort to deal with its difficulties.

You can get a feel for an organization in a variety of ways: talk to their competitors; check with other companies that do business with them (suppliers, advertisers, etc.); contact associations to learn about the company's public relations; check with the Chamber of Commerce; and also, tap into your own network for information. Knowledge of company trends and challenges (as it relates to your skills) is also valuable to build into your marketing letter.

Researching and gathering information about a company can boost your confidence going into the screening interviews. This knowledge provides an easy, and likely impressive, focus for discussion with the interviewers.

Presentation

After all the effort you have put into personal and environmental analyses, you will be well prepared to showcase your strengths—able to approach an interview situation or present a resume with confidence. The examples chosen to highlight your accomplishments will also help you identify your significant job skills and core behaviors—and, in particular, those which relate to the new position or job.

If possible, try to secure some form of job description before the interview so that you know which examples are most appropriate. This information will enable you to tailor your presentation using your SARBs to address the needs that are being sought. The presentation will also include work history, where you were employed, titles held, and what responsibilities were assigned to you.

As part of the interview process, you may be meeting with people from several different departments. For instance, for a position in production, you may have to meet with people from sales, marketing and finance. Since the position will have an impact on other parts of the company—you need to be able to tailor the presentation to address the needs of these different groups—match your strengths to their needs.

In most cases you will feel comfortable describing yourself in several ways, again depending on the nature of the opportunity. Often the interviewer gets focused on skills (e.g. accounting, management, sales, technical/ operations), however, your personal characteristics or behaviors, are an important component for company interviewers to recognize. Note that the interviewer won't ask you about behaviors, but, in some manner, will ask about strengths.

Use your behaviors to deliver a powerful response; this chart provides examples:

Personal Behaviors
(more examples in *Coaches Corner*):

Interpersonal skills	Organization/ planning	Flexible
Strategic thinking	Communication	Adaptable
Creative	Persistence	Focused
Team work	Perspective	High energy
Accountable	Self-directed	Motivation

Perseverance	Leadership	Consistent
Problem-solving	Decision making	Reflective

Behaviors like creativity, leadership, flexibility, and persistence, for instance, can be easily highlighted in your SARB presentation—or an employer may seek decision-making abilities and because of your examination, you can readily provide evidence for this.

Values, habits and attitudes are less perceptible and may not be clearly evident to others, but you must ensure these come across loud and clear to the interviewer. If you have used the SARB process to develop vignettes, you will be prepared to relate your values or attitudes in any given situation.

To be able to share your values in a job search will add depth to your presentation. In today's world of work, taking active responsibility for your own career increases the likelihood you'll achieve greater satisfaction, challenge, and overall employability in your own company and the employment marketplace.

A serious career examination takes time and effort—it also demands self-motivation and focus; you want to be able to make informed decisions about the direction of your career. The plan we have described will leave you with valuable information:

- a thorough knowledge of your job skills, attitudes, values, and behaviors;

- comprehensive intelligence about the work environments to which you are best suited; and,

- a framework to amalgamate your information into effective presentations for a new department or company.

Once you have amassed all this valuable knowledge and recognize the benefits of an examination—don't stop there—organize your plan so you can be a life-long learner.

Career Examination

Questions to Ask Yourself

- What behaviors motivate me?
- Which behaviors do I use?
- Where do I want to work?
- What are my SARBs?

OK, I need knowledge of what I am selling
to map a career route.

Chapter 3

There is a vitality, a life force, an energy, a quickening, that is translated through you into action, and because there is only one of you in all time, this expression is unique. And if you block it, it will never exist through any other medium and will be lost.
Martha Graham

Accomplishments - Roadmap To A New Job

THE PATH TO A new opportunity starts with what is important to you now and what you have to offer the job market in the future. You have revisited your interests, identified your strengths and behaviors; the next step is to recall and develop accomplishment statements to support your career progress.

It has been our experience while coaching, that often people find it difficult to recall the value of their contributions made to the company—at least initially: *I was just doing my job.* In most positions, many things that were important to the company are noted only briefly as our careers progress. These accomplishments are the best possible foundation to build upon and use to demonstrate to potential employers the difference you made while in your previous employment.

> Accomplishments are the evidence you need to illustrate that you can work effectively, have the can-do skills and demonstrate how you have benefited your employer. Accomplishment statements are the answers to interview questions.

While advising clients, we always suggested that they start with a simple "Chronology of Employment": where you were employed, the dates you worked there, company titles, and briefly, what tasks and responsibilities were required of you. This is time well spent—it will help you to identify your behaviors, construct your resume and later, assist during interviews.

In the event that you do choose to have someone prepare the resume professionally, remember you have to supply the data, and in the interviews, you will have to recall this information—know why you chose every single word in the resume. We found that clients who took time to develop and think through the accomplishments that demonstrate their behaviors, secured employment faster. Why? Because of their efforts, they were able to speak confidently and knowledgeably about themselves.

To begin developing your accomplishment statements, think in terms of contributions you and your colleagues made while solving problems, so that your position or functional area could operate smoothly. Some examples are:

- improved operations or made things run smoother and with more productivity
- achieved goals with fewer resources
- managed a project for a new undertaking

- improved customer service
- met or exceeded quality standards
- took the initiative to solve a problem that no one else was tackling
- wrote procedures and new polices that saved time and money
- hired and trained employees with low turnover
- introduced a new program/ undertaking, such as computerizing inventory
- preparation of reports, business publications, or documents
- delivered computer-based training
- increased sales or profits – improved quality – reduced expenses – reorganized a system.

Accomplishment Statements

When writing about accomplishments, you are looking for specific information; your statement will usually have five aspects in common:

1. Start the accomplishment statement with an action verb (e.g. achieved, improved, increased).
2. Describe what took place.
3. Describe the action or situation.
4. A good rule of thumb is to always try to show how the action benefited the organization in one or more ways.
   - cost savings
   - improved efficiencies
   - increased revenue

NOTE: *always try to state results/ changes quantifiably.*

5. What did I use to get the job done?
   - behaviors

- job knowledge
- attitude

While coaching clients through the development of their accomplishments and identifying their behaviors, it was especially rewarding to observe the transition from *Who's going to hire me?* to being *Proud and Anxious* to present themselves to companies with the confidence that they can discuss their strengths and behaviors in the interview—*I really have something to offer a company.*

The other obvious outcome of written accomplishments is being able to incorporate them into the resume to demonstrate strengths and accomplishments. Of course it will help in presenting yourself to the interviewer. We learned from our recruiter network something that wasn't very surprising to us as coaches: a large percentage of applicants were just not prepared to discuss their background using specific accomplishments. Most tried to rely on platitudes like . . . *I love working with people; I really like working with teams.* Be more direct than that.

Some people may find it difficult to recall all of the strengths and behaviors used to achieve success. When trying to apply the process of developing accomplishments you need to consider this: you may have acquired a long track record of successes by repetition—some of your skills are used automatically. You may have just forgotten you have them! On occasion some clients believed that behaviors, etc. were innate talents, but things like communication, planning, decision-making and managing are cultivated over time and with practice.

Examples of Accomplishment Statements for a Resume

In many cases when you insert an accomplishment statement into your resume it can be condensed to 18 – 21 words without losing its impact. See the examples below:

- Increased production by 20% and saved $250,000 in operating expenses.
- Increased sales by 9% though development of new

product seminars.

- Created quick response communication system resulting in an 18% increase of consumer deposits.
- Reduced receivables from 45 days to 30 days.

The goal has always been to be very brief—you want the reader to wonder how it was accomplished and be induced to ask for more details; once the reader is curious, you have gained his attention—and you have an interview!

Examples of Using Behaviors to Answer a Question

Question: *Explain your role as a team leader.*
Answer: Well, as the leader of a group I believe that everyone will perform better, function properly if they have an appreciation of why we are doing a particular project or work in general. As the leader, I take the time to communicate with them, answer their questions and solicit their comments, and where possible, showcase the use of their ideas. In promoting teamwork and cooperation in almost all situations, a cohesive work group is created and their interest grows in their work and themselves.

> *-showcases: being a leader, getting it done with people, communicator, listening skills and participative skills*

Question: *How are you best managed?*
Answer: I have always prided myself on staying informed and on top of my department plans and goals to support the corporate objectives or issues to be resolved. When I say 'staying informed' that means continuing to enhance my business acumen, staying knowledgeable in current and future possibilities. By being informed as well as being comfortable around senior management I am recognized as a get-it-done manager. I like to be managed by giving me a general picture of what needs to happen, specific needs, tell me why we are headed in a particular direction and your expectations plus any reports required. Then turn me loose.

> *-showcases: planning, business acumen, comfort at senior levels, staying informed, direction to take, working on your own*

Note: The two examples above do not contain a specific event and result. The professional interviewer will most likely follow-up with a situational question request like: *Can you give me an example?*

You would then select an accomplishment related to the situation and deliver the answer. Remember the SARB is your answer to an interview question.

Question: *Can you describe for me a situation where you were under a lot of stress to perform with a difficult deadline?*
Answer: Yes I can. I had just started with a new employer as the Employment Manager. My responsibilities included employment, medical department, the cafeteria and the training department. I was on the job for two days when my boss came in and informed me; "You are making a presentation to the Chairmen of the Board, at the Union Club this coming Saturday" –which was four days away. My boss was going to be out of town during the period so I had no fall-back. *(situation)*

I immediately summoned the department heads into a planning meeting, set the tone by laying out a variety of issues, and asked for their help. I learned that the main reason for the presentation was that the bank's senior management was planning a symposium. I then detailed a functional informational gathering plan with due times (not dates) for completion. *(action)*

As a team we put together a presentation that included the past circumstance of each department, the future projects, corporate action plans and how these were supported by our level of performance in accomplishing them, and some key points about our future needs. I kept my job, made some friends quickly, Chairman was pleased which meant my boss was pleased. *(result)*

The reason this was a success is that I feel I have excellent coping abilities and can maintain a mature problem-solving attitude while dealing with stressful situations. (*behavior*)

---

behaviors used: coping, tolerance for ambiguity, decisiveness, communications and leadership

---

Some basic coaching advice: Don't focus solely on grand spectacular achievements. *Consistent performance in your job* may not sound noteworthy to you, but it is recognized by employers. You can also demonstrate behaviors by utilizing significant accomplishments made in the community.

Regardless of the approach you take, the importance of concise, results-oriented accomplishment statements is essential for your job search campaign. It will better prepare you, help the resume writing, the interview process, and will distinguish you from the other job seekers. Knowing your skills and behaviors will help you to market yourself to targeted companies as well as any employers you are referred to from your networking.

Roadmap to a New Job

Questions to Ask Yourself:

• Have I carefully identified my SARBs? especially behavior?

• Do I see how SARBs guide the interview?

• Will the SARBs I've chosen build my confidence?

My references said what?!!!

Chapter 4

The only people you should ever want to get "even with"
are those who have helped you.
John Honeyfeld

REFERENCES:
What Will People Say About You?

PROACTIVE MANAGEMENT OF YOUR references is the best way to maximize their impact on your job campaign and convince the employer you are as good as you say.

Most former bosses, associates, subordinates and customers you would consider for your *References List* will welcome the opportunity to help you. Think about who will make a useful reference:

- supervisors/ superiors who have direct knowledge of

your activities;
- upper level management;
- co-workers;
- staff that you have supervised;
- suppliers, clients;
- personal references.

Identify References

We always advised our clients to make early contact with their references—the moment the decision is made to enter the market. Support is crucial early on in the job search and references should be identified before too much time is lost. They can help you with the discovery phase—how they see you.

Once you have identified the references, talk to them, get their permission and tell them you will get back to them to share your work search plans and a copy of your resume. It is your responsibility to prepare references to reinforce the knowledge and behaviors you are selling. It is also advisable to share with references what you want to accomplish, ask for their advice and see if they are willing to be part of your "Job Search Board of Directors." They may also have some contacts that they want to share with you.

Stay in touch with the references as you move through the job search; they should be kept informed and brought up-to-date on new events, new contacts, surprises, etc. every ten days.

Reference Statement

It's important to have a prepared reference statement (a "Tell Me About Yourself" answer) that your references should use as a guideline (the Background Overview will work well—see *Coaches Corner XI*).

Once you have your resume, send it to your references; it is also a good idea to ask for their opinion of it. By asking for their opinion, you are assured that your references will have read your resume. It is also a good idea to ensure that their recollections of you, your work and achievements coincide with what you are saying about your background, work history or accomplishments and behaviors. Share your prepared reference statement with them and ask for their personal thoughts.

In most interview situations you will be asked several probing questions about your working relationship with former bosses.

> Work out an "official statement" to
> address why you left or why you
> are thinking about leaving.

Now it could be that the reason you have left was a negative relationship with your supervisor; it happens. This is a big red flag for an interviewer/ employer. It's worth the time to work out a neutral ground with your former boss or sometimes you can get another manager in the company to give you a reference and lessen the impact. However, if you had an unsatisfactory working relationship, it is important to examine why the relationship was difficult. Be able to demonstrate how, and what you have learned from the experience—turn a negative into something positive.

If you were released, construct a story about why, and what was learned from the situation. In the case of inadequate knowledge, talk about how the job changed, what was missing and what is being done about it now. Perhaps personalities did not mesh—this is usually a matter of behaviors not meshing; talk about initiatives and what types of people you work best with.

If your references are willing to be on your job search board, certainly keep them informed without being a pest. You may just want to e-mail everyone else status reports. They may also have network contacts to refer to you or someone who might benefit your search.

Additional Referencing

Job seekers need to be aware of some additional referencing. The use of third party organizations that are paid by companies to do a background check(s) on final candidates for a job is becoming more popular in today's job market. What the company may want verified will depend on the type of position and level of authority.

> The company must give you a separate form to sign stating they plan to do this additional referencing. Note that when you sign the application, you are only attesting that everything on the application is true and factual—the company must have you sign a release form in order to pursue third party background checks.

Managing References

Handling Poor References

If you are aware of and feel that a critical reference may not agree with the results you reference, you can do a couple of things. When discussing this reference with a potential employer, state that these were the circumstances from your perspective and possible reasons why you may not get a good review from this person. You may suggest why this person might feel that way. Depending on the circumstances, several of our clients actually met with the reference and got an agreement to state something beyond the disagreements that existed, keeping it work-related.

When you are engaged in networking with a recruiter she may ask you for your references. You have to be careful in complying, as she may want to use your contacts to further her marketing activities. A good response is simply that: you understand the need to verify your information and you will provide your references once you become a candidate for a job.

> Maintain some reference control because
> you don't want your references to burnout
> (e.g. by receiving a lot of calls).

It is very critical to take action when there is a job offer or when you are a finalist. Alert references to expect a call; advise them of pertinent job details and the factors you want them to emphasize about your background. Ask that they notify you after being called so you can learn what questions were asked and what was discussed. Sometimes people are hired without the references being verified until later. In this case, take the same contact action steps—however, state that you have been hired and started. Don't let this step go by the wayside.

Making your reference program part of your search campaign is a great way to sometimes help wrap-up the position when in a close race with another candidate.

Once hired and settled into a new position, it is time to contact your network and others involved in the job search. Be sure to send your references a sincere thank-you note and in some cases a small token of appreciation for their help. Offer to serve as a reference for them if needed. If there have been some good recruiters involved, advise them about your new job. Finally, it is important to contact your network—you want to keep them informed. Send some form of communication and enclose two business cards. Besides keeping them up-to-date, maintain your network for potential future needs.

Reference Lists

Most reference lists will contain, at a minimum, the following information:
- person to whom you reported
- past employer
- professional peer
- professional not associated with your job who can be a personal character reference
- in sales, a customer/ major account you serviced
- staff member

Perhaps you have received something in writing from a boss, customer, an award, etc. Make copies to give out at the appropriate interview time. DON'T mail them with your resume, as they will not have the same impact on the recruiter; instead, hand them out during the interview to solidify a point.

Managing references is a vital part of any job search and strong references are one more key to securing a position. Establish a list, solicit their opinion and assistance, and work with them to achieve your goals. And don't forget to express your appreciation after the fact—you may need to call on them in the future.

Note: *Sample reference worksheet in*
Coaches Corner VI

References

Questions to Ask Yourself

- What is my plan for gathering the best references?
- How will I approach my references to get their assistance?
- How will I keep my references informed?

How will I create value for a company?

Chapter 5

Genuine beginnings begin within us,
even when they are brought to our
Attention by external opportunities.
William Bridges

Are You Ready to Sell Yourself?

NOW DON'T PANIC (especially if you have never held a sales position)! Actually this chapter can be divided into two parts; "Are You Ready?" and "Selling Yourself." Let's start with selling. When you think about selling what is it that comes to mind? The dictionary defines sell as: to exchange (e.g. goods and services) for money or its equivalent. When a sales call is defined or discussed it will usually consist of:

- a presentation of a product/ service;

- learn about or create a need for the product;
- develop a want or a desire for the product;
- overcome objections if raised; and
- close or ask for the business.

Let's convert the product/service in the sales call to your background or YOU as the product. Think about the similarities:

- Do you make a presentation to the interviewer?
- Do you want to create a need for your skills?
- Do you develop expectations in reviewing your accomplishments?
- Do you overcome objections by discussing your behaviors?
- Do you ask what are the next steps?

The answer to all of the above is yes! So everyone is capable of selling themselves. Right, Ron? You will be working with a product that you know better than anyone, in terms of what you can do - will do - want to do.

Are You Ready? It is more than having a resume or feeling confident about interviewing. *Being Ready* means much more. Let's take a look some areas you may not have considered:

- Have you discussed being out of work with your family? your friends? Being a first time job seeker is scary, as are moves to a different job and seeking advancement within the same company. Getting past the initial embarrassments is very important.
- Do you have your emotions in control? Are you past the anger of *Why Me*?
- Are you willing to do the work necessary for you to get the job you want?
- Do you have a financial plan to determine how long you can be out of work or how long you can be in the present position . . . and then what?

- Where are you going to conduct your research? Do you have a library card? (Don't laugh! In a class of 20 people we offered $5.00 for the first person who produced a library card. Guess what? Maybe 2-3 people had a card.)
- What are your computer skills like? Maybe you need to consider taking a refresher class?

We know there are other topics to consider but the above list includes the more prevalent areas we have seen with our clients.

One client we worked with was so embarrassed about being out of work that he never told his wife and family. He got up every morning and proceeded to go to work as he always did. He drove to our offices and worked on his re-employment plan and then went home as if coming from work. Emotionally he was wired.

It didn't last very long. As we got wind of what was taking place, we worked with him to overcome the embarrassment of losing his job so he could move on to telling his wife and family. He secured a job and as he was saying his goodbyes to us, he said the experience of having to look for a job had greatly improved his outlook on life.

Some folks would say things happen for a reason. That may be so, but another way to look at life is: there are two things we don't control (1) being born (2) when we die. So, everything else in-between we control. We write our destiny every day by the decisions we make.

Now, getting back to: *Are You Ready?* Do you have a *public reason* for leaving your job (e.g. company has been sold, company had undergone downsizing—reasons that are *publicly* known versus personal)? If you have not considered this or if you are expecting to be highly recruited and grabbed up by a company, you will most likely have to adjust your thinking. In today's job market, and most likely for the foreseeable future, securing employment opportunities will continue to be very competitive. This is the century that most industries across the board will work towards smaller staffs with solid skills who achieve higher productivity.

The person who can communicate her behaviors in presentations will, in most cases, be the winner.

Exit Statement

Develop an exit statement (as part of your presentation) to explain why you are available for employment in another company. If you are still employed and you are searching to make an employment move you will need a specific and logical justification about *why*.

For example: you want to change because of a business reason or career growth opportunities; even if there is an opportunity to be recruited by a professional search firm you still need an exit statement.

Why are you willing to leave if it's a good job? Developing a business reason for leaving (as opposed to a personal reason) is more accepted and less controversial for marketing/presenting yourself for employment opportunities.

Avoid:
- didn't get along with the boss;
- couldn't advance my career;
- the culture changed around me;
- worked too hard—burned out;
- didn't want to relocate (okay for a regional company).

Having a positive statement will also be more acceptable to verify (references) by your former company.

Business reasons:
- advancing my career;
- reduction in force;
- acquisition/ merger—redundant position
- reorganization;
- new management/ new team (why didn't you fit in?);

- headquarters moved—projects outsourced, less need for my skills.

There may be situations where there is a personal reason (for instance, new skills, high education position/ duties) and references can really help in confirming the situation. It's best to state your business reason rather than giving the interviewer a reason for sensing a red flag. Keep your explanation brief, factual and make sure that you can support it in your references.

Setting-the-Stage

Once you have settled on an exit statement and tested it with your business associates, it's time to begin developing your 1-2 minute setting-the-stage presentation. The questions, *Tell me about yourself* or *Give me a brief overview of your career,* are commonly used to start the interview—this is the warm-up or setting-the-stage.

The interviewer is asking for two things upfront: *how prepared does this person appear* and *how poised is the applicant?* These questions have a way of appearing in other areas as well. For instance, when networking, the person you network with may begin the conversation with similar questions.

Keep your presentation short. Most people are conditioned to listen or pay attention for about 20-30 seconds. Why? We are conditioned by commercials on TV, which are 30 seconds in length. As we discussed in the previous chapter, a good format to begin with is:

- early years;
- education;
- military (if any);
- then progressive job responsibility, up to most recent job.

Here is an example of another approach to discuss your career, accomplishments and education/specialized training:

After graduating from Michigan State University, I started my career in human resources, covering the hospitality, technical, and financial industries. The last ten years were spent with United Bank of Arizona. One of my key accomplishments during that period was my success in creating an atmosphere, which held turnover to a level below national averages. I was selected to attend the Financial Executive Program at the University of Washington. This program covered all senior management positions, primarily CEO, Senior Ops jobs and management of commercial banks.

Then go on to demonstrate knowledge: *After researching the company's Web site and my initial understanding of the position, I believe my job knowledge could benefit the position by . . .* and give an example. At first this sounds like a short story about you—that is exactly what you don't want this to become! Start with the end objective in mind and then just work towards that goal. If you have fifteen years plus work experience, you may want to start with your most recent job. By breaking down the presentation as we suggested, you will be able to deliver a good presentation—no matter what the interviewer asks or where he starts. Don't try to memorize as it is easy to get lost, then likely you would have to start all over again. How embarrassing!

The best way to really feel comfortable with your presentation is to videotape it and try using different facial expressions, movements, pauses, and so on. We did say setting the *stage*, didn't we! Seriously, this form of practice will build confidence and help to impress the interviewer.

Think about it. How much fun is it to be an interviewer with, on the average, 15-20 or more openings to recruit for? The average response to a good position can be 700-800 applicants. This times 10 (the recruiting would probably be staggered) is approximately 8500 resumes in hard copy, on the Website and even faxed. The numbers need to be pared down to 20-25 prospects and use phone screens with those who seem the most promising.

Once she has the most qualified 5-7 applicants for the position, she normally will run the resumes past the hiring manager to get his opinion. All things being good to go, the recruiter will probably do a phone interview to get more details and decide who qualifies (perhaps 2 applicants) to come to the company for an interview. What happens to the rest of the resumes? The recruiter may keep several on file that look good for some other position or for backup, and the others (if we are lucky) receive a *thanks, but not today* card or letter. To give you some idea about just how many resumes or applications are floating in the sea of resumes:

- An article in *US News and World Report* states that typically 1000 unsolicited resumes arrive in the daily mail at Fortune 500 companies and 80% are tossed out after a quick perusal!

- Internet recruitment companies like monster.com and hotjobs.com receive thousands of resumes daily.

- On their website, careerbuilders.com state that they add over 15,000 new resumes daily for a total of 10 million plus registered resumes.

How many search engines are out there? How will you be remembered? I think you would agree now that setting-the-stage is very important!

Getting Prepared

Let's back up a little in the sequence of events and deal with how you got the interview opportunity. The network you have developed will more often than not generate the interview opportunity (visit networking section in *Coaches Corner*).

You have investigated and researched the company. As well, you have identified your strengths and ideal work environment. You will have prepared a *briefing book* (company reference book you prepare—discussed fully in Chapter 8) that you can take to the interview and use as a reference tool. In the initial investigation of the company, you have assessed the financials (if this is not a strength of yours, get help). As well, read the editorial in the company's annual report and/ or check out the company with the Chamber of Commerce. This information will serve a base for questions you may want to ask during the interview(s). The personal objective is to know more about the company than the people you may visit with during the interview process (and don't be surprised—as this is easier than it sounds!).

Find out about 10-K, 401K matching history, changes in the benefit coverages, your costs—these are a good indicator of what the company is like; they may say that they are people-oriented, but actions speak louder. This type of information is also valuable when you get to the offer. Your research should also tell you what the competition is like, about plans for R & D and new products/ market share.

This is just a small sample of the picture you are painting. You should find annual salaries of the officers, personal bios, and how much downsizing or outsourcing of jobs overseas they have done.

> A benefit of these actions is a significant gain of confidence—your comfort level increases with knowledge and prepares the path for better-informed interview delivery on your part.

Now, as the interview day approaches, someone from the company calls you to confirm the place and time of the interview. You should be prepared to ask this person several things:

- the type of interview structure being used (behavioral, screening, panel, one-on-one, etc.);
- who you are meeting with, along with their titles;
- what is the timeframe for each interview;
- will you need to fill out an application? and,
- a job description (if you don't have one).

In this series of potential interview meetings, you have equipped yourself with enough knowledge that there is no way you can mess this up! Remember people hire people so don't enter this arena of battle with an attitude; you still have to sell them on you and your fit.

Third Party Interventions – Recruiters – Search Firms

If you happen to be represented by a search firm or a recruiter, you may wonder: can this be a good thing? For the person still employed, it is a good strategy to work solely with a recruiting firm. This way, the question of why the person is leaving is already covered by the recruiter and the company. Some things to consider:

(1) the recruiter should be equipped with information about the position;

(2) the recruiter is paid by the company—remember who they work for;

(3) recruiters should have company knowledge, hiring authority priorities, inside knowledge about why the position is open, and in their opinion, what it may take to be successful in this position.

(You can find further information on different forms of third party help in *Coaches Corner III*)

Actually, what you are doing is planning your interview strategy with them. Search firms that are successful usually get repeat business from the company to bring qualified applicants to their attention. If this is not the case, maybe you should tell them to take a hike! OK, not really, but be sure you are comfortable with the firm that represents you in the market. Good prospecting!

Are You Ready to Sell Yourself?

Questions to Ask Yoursef:

• Why am I seeking new work?

• What is my emotional state?

• Are all my bases covered?

Now let's see. Which key shows the answer to:
Why Shouldn't We Hire You?

Veek © 2007

Chapter 6

Our only security is our ability to change.
John Lilly

INTERVIEWING

Something about interviews and interviewers

The time has finally arrived—the interview—the opportunity for which you have been preparing. You have been thinking about questions that may be asked and practicing your responses learned from interview books, right? It is the first chance you've had to collectively bring your search to a critical point and you are now on your home field. **No one knows more about what you can do than you!** *Your emotions are going to be heightened at this time; you have a solid awareness of yourself, you feel good about all that you have accomplished, mentally you are in your comfort zone, your game plan is ready, and now you can carry out your plan. Don't confuse the* *interview with a psychiatrist's session and don't let the emotions of the transition creep back in. This is what you have rehearsed; you are conducting an orchestrated event*: **the interview.**

The Interview

THE JOB INTERVIEW IS always the prime focus of the re-employment or search process. It's a series of discussions in which you have the opportunity to gain an understanding of the company. In turn, the interviewers will be measuring the benefits that you bring to the company/ position and will want to determine if there is a fit into their team and culture. Although you want the majority of your interviews to be conducted as one-on-one with the decision makers, today there is a process where most interviews start with a phone screening.

Once you get past the screening interview there is a strong trend toward team interviews. This technique, called group interviewing, is used by companies to save time and still get maximum exposure to the candidate. The group interview usually involves at least 2-3 employees who conduct the session, often: someone from human resources, the department hiring manager, and someone from outside the department. The content of the interview is usually the same as a one-to-one meeting, except there are three people asking prepared questions:

- in their areas of interest—as your work will impact them;
- general questions and specific job knowledge—thus the depth of your job knowledge;
- getting a picture of the real you (your behaviors).

Friend, Foe or Just Another Challenge in Life

You are in control and can make the interview event your friend—there is no foe unless you create one by being unprepared and not really knowing yourself. Through observation of clients, we have noted that many people do not like to interview; they are apprehensive about what questions will be asked, and overwhelmingly, *people just don't like talking about themselves.* They can talk about what they do but have a difficult time talking about who they are.

Some of this apprehension has to do with the circumstances around getting to the interview. If you left your last job involuntarily, make sure that your emotional state is in order before any attempt to engage in interviewing. At the initial stage of a job loss and personal transition you do not want to overreact or panic about not having a job. It is a good idea to hold off from making any initial contacts with targeted companies, job positions or networking with people until you are ready emotionally.

> Even if you have had the unfortunate experience
> of being downsized several times, spend time
> getting prepared to present yourself in the most
> favorable light to the needs of the company.

Depending upon your situation in life, both personal- and work-related knowledge can have an impact on your career prospects. Today we know that doing a good job is not enough to keep it. Our employment prospects can change for reasons that have nothing to do with quality of a job done. It's a new economy, with new rules, measurements, and different working values than we operated with earlier in our working experiences. The global economy has brought about many changes: outsourcing of jobs (even parts of jobs) domestically as well as globally, and redeployment has become more common. The faster we embrace the changes, the better position we will be in to control our future.

If you left a position due to job performance or related issue, you will have to figure out how to respond to the *why* of that situation.

> Then prepare—prepare—prepare and
> practice—practice—practice
> the answers to: *why did you leave?*

A similar situation occurs when a person leaves a position due to downsizing—the question then is: *why didn't they keep you*? It is critical that you are prepared for these questions—because they will be asked. This might be the perfect time to demonstrate your ability to learn and grow—if you can describe the situation under which you left a previous company and what you learned from it, or how it has changed your priorities—you can turn a negative situation into something very constructive. An example follows:

> I was on a recruiting trip in Orno, Maine and the next day I had to be at the University of Pittsburgh. A snowstorm came in grounding all air traffic. I called the office and asked if someone else could go to Pittsburgh—no one could. So I rode a bus from Orno to Boston, and arrived around 5AM. I was dead tired and decided to rent a room for a three-hour period before boarding my flight to Pittsburgh.

> Well my company, a government contractor, thought it was poor judgment to spend money on a room as I could have waited and flown to Pittsburgh, cleaned up there and rested on the flight before my interviews. They said I lost my effectiveness because of poor judgment. Now because of this, I think through more deeply any time financial matters are involved and, in fact, all of my concentrated thinking about problems is as a result of this incident.

You will need references from someone to verify your work.

The statement, *It was a mutual agreement*, is received in most interviews with suspicion.

It's a big red flag when an interviewer asks for the name of your last reporting relationship and you say something like, *Oh she or he won't give me a good reference . . .* next in line please. Unfortunately there may be circumstances that will not appear positive to the listener if you don't provide details to explain your position. Consider this, employers are not in the business of keeping you unemployed. Sit down with them and work out a reference upon which you both agree.

In Jack Welch's book, *Jack* (2001), he states when he looked to hire someone he looked for the person who was fired at least once. This may sound odd, but there is a school of thought that sees this as a potentially positive thing—being fired once will provide an employer with the opportunity to see how this person learns from past mistakes. Another is that when a person has been fired once, she is certainly not going to let it happen again—so the person is going to be a better worker!

There are other driving forces to the changing workforce, just to mention a few: we are living longer, have healthier life-styles and more interests, are better educated, and there is also the influence of global economics. As we add up all the forces, employees are becoming aware that they must take responsibility for their career direction. Some folks can see that they need to be flexible, self-aware employees who continually seek to improve their skills. Gone are the days of being employed by the same organization for a 30-year career. If it happens, good, but we will predict that even though you have stayed with the same organization, you were still required to look (and interview) for new positions or move to new challenges within the organization. There are no safe harbors.

FAB: Features, Advantages, Benefits

Workers of today and tomorrow need to learn how *not* to be dependent upon just one employer. In order to have choices, you want to learn how to market your career proactively. Companies who develop a new product brand it or market it to the best potential consumer. The same is true for you, except you are the product, and you will be always watchful for opportunities to present your **FAB**—acronym for the concept of you as the **product**:

- FEATURES are your key job knowledge and key behaviors
- ADVANTAGES of your experiences—SARB statements
- how you can BENEFIT the company

Changing Job Environment

In order to stay ahead of the game, you must research and determine what skills are going to be needed to fit into the new directions potential employers are taking and industries are evolving. All employees need to understand the value of self-education in order to become more valuable for employers or new opportunities. Coasting in a job is a good path for being declared excess; snooze and you will lose.

Some of you reading this book will be the leaders of this changing environment for the workforce: ME, INC. We already know that technology has impacted our way of doing business and that people's careers are being changed by technology more than any one event to-date. This will continue at an even faster pace with new jobs that require new skill sets. These events and more will also affect your attitude towards having a sense of security. In the past having tenure and feeling that you were part of a company made you feel secure. That is not necessarily the situation today; people have to create their own security by knowing who they are and that they are very employable—people are in charge of themselves and control their career destiny.

The upside of this change is that everyone has an opportunity to take charge of their employment career direction now.

People use swimming coaches to improve skills, trainers work with us to better our health or even our golf game—we should also consider services of a career coach.

The professional career coach will help identify where to modify career direction to fit your needs or skills, and importantly, can advise about the ever-changing job market. When we decided to write a book dealing with the interview, this decision was based upon what we believed to be the best way to help individuals in the process of career management and competing in a job search.

The contributing factors to the potential career directions a person may want to exercise are both within reason and endless. Think about it or better yet, just look at your own situation and how you are deciding which career path to follow. You need to sort through volumes of information to plan the direction you might want to take, right? In fact, we found that there was one factor that remained the most consistent throughout all of these systems of change—a person still needs to be a good interviewer (skilled at participating in the interview process). People will, approximately 83% of the time, perform as they have in the past. If you want to change, the one option is to modify this action by replacing a poor behavior with a good behavior.

Preparation is Crucial

Remember we said that it has been our experience that the best jobs don't always go to who would appear to be the person with the most job knowledge. It often gets down to the individuals who are better prepared for the interview—that is, those who know who they are in terms of work knowledge and behaviors. They win more *you're hired* answers in the selection process. *Skilled interviewees* have a real ability to plan successful job searches, find the "best fit" employers and manage their career. The better you are able to present your strengths, understand that behaviors and interests impact your ability to get work done, the more solid your job search foundation.

As you reach the place and time to begin the interviews, remember that there may be many other candidates who are competing for the job. They too could be anxious, but unless they have read this book they will probably experience even more anxiety and not be sufficiently prepared.

A good book to add to your reading list is *The Power of Focus* (2000) by Jack Canfield, Mark Victor Hansen and Les Hewitt. It is a clear, simple, roadmap that shows how to focus on what is important in your life as well as career.

In the screening and initial one-to-one interviews, the interviewers are looking to see whether you qualify as a member of the *to be considered* or the *not interested* applicant flow—the selection is mostly based on job knowledge at this point.

With the reduction of available jobs, it goes without saying that the interview process used by companies today, and in the future, will be competitive and challenging, especially if you haven't been involved with the process in the last five years. This scenario will still be prevalent as the shift to a seller's environment (more jobs than skilled people to fill them) continues. If you want to read more about the economy of tomorrow, look for Futurist author Alvin Toffler's published works.

If you are one of the few fortunate long-term employees, to compete in today's job market you will definitely need to spend time rethinking your interview knowledge and skills, and the salary level you are most likely in love with. Until the market changes to where there are more jobs than applicants, in order to secure a better job that has some future, today's job search applicant needs to understand branding/ packaging of his job knowledge. This is one technique to use in presenting your professional expertise more effectively than ever before (the *Branding* subject is covered in *Coaches Corner*).

General Guidelines for Interview Responses

When answering questions, keep several guidelines in mind. First and foremost keep your answers short and concise as you cover the subject with specific terms, including behaviors and results—the interview answer should be done in about 1.5 to 2 minutes maximum. If the interviewer wants more detail, she will guide you in that direction. Monologues or lectures as part of the delivery will only burn up valuable interview time, will easily lose the interviewer's interest and have a way of creating an unfavorable impression. It's like reading a magazine or the newspaper—the headline usually sums up the story, first paragraph condenses the whole story, with the major facts coming early and the more detailed or trivial information is found at the end.

The company Web site should be visited and you need to have some feel for the financials. In today's job market not having the time to learn about the company is not an acceptable excuse. A success-oriented applicant will use the interview to show more than that he is seeking a specific position—he will use it to demonstrate an excellent track record of accomplishments and that he is prepared to perform in the position and adapt to the company's culture. Simply put, you are investigating the opportunity and marketing yourself at the same time.

We will visit the different types of potential interviews later, but regardless of the style of questioning you enter into, never allow yourself to go to an interview with an employer, or a recruiter retained by a company, without arming yourself with two things:

- as much knowledge as possible about the organization; and,
- as much knowledge as possible about who and what you are selling.

The main reason you have been invited for an interview is that the employer saw something she liked in your experience as presented in the resume, network referral or the results of a pre-screening interview. Your ability to develop rapport and trust will be as important as behaviors and track record (accomplishments). Your qualifications may have been the driving force that got you to the interview—but remember, the person who presents themselves well usually wins. Always be prepared to build your knowledge of the company's business issues, and how you can impact those issues, into the discussion.

Types of Interviews

The *informational interview* can be a formal or informal discussion mainly for the purpose of securing information to decide on further courses of action. This form of meeting is synonymous with a career change objective or with a network meeting and is usually arranged and conducted by the job seeker.

A company uses *screening interviews* to screen you in or out based on predetermined qualifications or criteria. Professional recruiters, internal human resource professionals and in some cases, the hiring manager use this technique to identify the applicants that they feel are qualified—that is, determine the depth and usage of knowledge as well as the behaviors of the applicants. Screening interviews also serve to save time and expense for the company.

In the *selection*, sometimes called *decision interviews*, the process is a planned, formal approach. It will contain more specific questioning that provides the interviewer with the information to evaluate whether a candidate has the *can do, will do, and fit* to perform successfully in the recruited position.

The trained interviewer conducting a structured interview will usually do the following:

- use open-ended questions and focus on demonstrable performances with behaviors using SARB;
- encourage the candidate to speak (85 percent of the meeting);
- either give a preview of the position or limit the information about the job until the candidate's qualifications have been confirmed.

Managing Your Emotions

An important note to remember, especially for those who may not be feeling positive about a job search—even though you feel your emotions are in control, sometimes anger will surface, especially during the interview process. You need to put the anger behind you or learn to simply use the energy as fuel to focus on the job search in a positive way. Anger is an important emotion as it demonstrates that you value yourself and the behaviors and job skills you bring to the potential position.

If you feel or find that you are not able to manage the anger, this may be a sign that several situations need attention in your life. Seek out some personal counseling so that you are able to deal with your feelings and focus on moving forward. The longer you are in the process of looking for a job the more likely it can create fear, or you begin feeling a loss of control. Fear can sometimes paralyze you into inactivity or it is the emotion that will sometimes cause you to project additional crises into your job search activities.

> Richard Bolles, author of *What Color Is Your Parachute?* (2003) in its 29th reprint, advises to never make negative statements about a former employer, regardless how tempting it may be. It will only set the stage for the interviewer to summarize that you could be a trouble maker, but also wonder what you will do if hired.

The bottom-line of the job search campaign is to get interviews, which should lead to job offers, then a position. It has been our experience that few individuals secure employment without participating in at least one (often more)interview. *Remember, while the long-range goal is to get the job offer, your immediate objective is to get the next interview.*

Interviewing

Questions to Ask Yourself:

- Will the interview be my friend?
- Have I clearly identify my FABs?
- Am I mentally clear about who I am?

Veek © 2007

I was supposed to ask questions!
What were they again?

Chapter 7

Ideas are a dime a dozen.
People who implement them are priceless.
Mary Kay Ash

The Call Comes for You to Interview

SO THE INTERVIEW CALL comes in asking you to inter-view and a date has been set. Congratulations! But now what? First consider this: there is no way you can go to an inter-view without having a good idea of what you will be talk-ing about. You have too much information readily available to help with planning. Bottom line, why do you think you got the call? Well, generally speaking, the only information the company has on you is your cover letter/ resume and the information it contains, or possibly the application you may have completed—so you will certainly be talking about these documents. Let's look at the resume. Have you studied your resume? Did you write it yourself? You must have planned out what you would say in a discussion about any work or statement, or even descriptors you have used on your re-sume—right?

Let's say, for instance, you described yourself as a *seasoned* administrative customer service manager. If asked about the word, *seasoned*, what are you going to say? Did you use seasoned because of your age? Perhaps you have something like *extensive* experience in materials management—what is the story behind *extensive*? How would you define *extensive*? Do you have an example thought out that would support the definition of *extensive*? The key point here is that you should be ready to discuss, in detail, every work experience on the resume as well as the descriptors used in the header—your resume is the roadmap for the interview.

> You must have a solid knowledge of yourself
> before heading into the interview.

SARB: Situation—Action—Results—Behavior

Ok, now that you have looked at your resume and know why or how you will support every word on it, let's go back to the business of not knowing what you're going to be talking about.

To begin, you have a recruiter on the phone; what comes to mind and what do you want to ask that person? You need to know location, time and whom you will be visiting with. Is it the decision maker or is it human resources or both? Each of those sessions involves a different mind-set in terms of the interview and typically, what will be asked should be differ-ent.

The questions should pertain to the area of responsibility and the linkage to the job. The HR folks want to verify the information on your resume and will most likely get a feel for your work behaviors. The decision maker is going to want to explore the depth of your skill base but more importantly, this person will explore what you are like to work with, again those behavioral rascals. While preparing to answer potential questions, don't overlook the SARB formula:

- What was the work: **Situation;**
- What **Action** did I take to solve or prevent the problem;
- What were the **Results** obtained; and
- **Behaviors**: the competencies statement, behaviors used.

*note: SARB was fully developed in Chapter 2

Ask the person on the phone if you could be sent a job description, or an annual report. You can also ask if the job is a new position and if so, why is it needed? Well, now you have gotten some information and you know the company's name, location of interview, time and have a feel for the type of questions that could be asked. Also, ask if a behavioral interview approach will be used.

By now you have reviewed, planned out answers to questions and thought about every word on your resume. Was there any information gained during this first phone call that you need to review? Your job now is to begin matching your background to that information. The presentation you develop demonstrates:

- why you should be considered for the job;
- what can be expected from you that benefits the company;
- how you fit into the team; and
- once again, visit your FAB.

So our thought here is that there is no way for you to get into an interview without knowing what you're going to be talking about. Also, it is a given that the company has an interest in you because of what is on your resume. You now know how to support the resume details and you also have research information; add to this the info gained during the screening interview via the phone—and you have more knowledge: **you are in the know!**

Other Sources of Information

Suppose you answered an advertisement—usually the ad contains basic information that provides you with an outline of what will be discussed. If you have a company name you are also able to visit the Web site and read about the organization. Suppose you are working with a recruiter—you can expect these folks will certainly have job information to which you can match your background. Let's say you only have the name of a company to deal with—research the company and determine what they are all about, products, and scope of activity. Then you can begin to match yourself to the company by looking at what they do.

Finally, what if you have nothing more than a job title? You have a network to source to see if anyone has information or knows someone who works at the company or in that same type of position. There are numerous recourses on the Internet for exploring job titles and you are able to get general descriptors so you can plan how your background fits that type of job.

The company's annual report—an important document. Any company will talk about themselves in somewhat glowing terms, but this is still helpful. Each one of those glowing terms is another opportunity for you to show, using your accomplishments and behaviors, how you fit the glowing terms. If the company is not publicly traded, there is the Chamber of Commerce. There may also be various associations, which would have information on local companies.

So, you will enter the interview knowledgeably! Now since you have a game plan, you have determined your core behaviors, and you have practiced discussing them as Situation—Action—Results—Behaviors (SARB) you are ready to make an effective and successful presentation. Good Luck!

Prepare!

What we have stressed again and again is that the most important aspect of interviewing is preparation. This process takes on many different forms and uses specific research resources.

- It is important to learn as much as possible about: the targeted company that has invited you to an interview, the position description, the interviewer(s) and as much information made available about what kind of person that they want to recruit.

- The amount of information that is available can be overwhelming, but if managed accordingly it can build your image and confidence in the interview process. Please refer to research resources in Coaches Corner.

Most applicants would like the interview to be conducted one-on-one with the decision makers, but in most companies today the interviews will typically start with a phone screen. You should always be prepared just in case you receive the phone call; however, if you are caught off guard there are a couple of things you can do. Remember the good news is that you made it through the paper screening and the company is interested in you.

If the call comes when you are not prepared ask if you could put him on hold for a few moments while you get to your office. Just in case you might get disconnected, get his phone number and check to see if it is a night number (most switchboards close at 5:00 pm).

- If you can delay the call then take a few minutes to review any information you have on the company or the position that you are applying for. This will help you be much better prepared and in a controlled state of mind which will help you to sell yourself for the job and get a chance to be invited into a face-to-face interview.

- It is important to have a quiet area in your home so you won't be distracted by noises or family activity. This includes making sure the dog is out of the room! A number of times clients have shared that their dog was quiet . . . until the phone interview.

- It is worth mentioning that you should be organized when the phone interview calls start coming. Do yourself a favor and develop a simple retrieval system of any information you have on the company or position for which you are applying, e.g./ alphabetical listing by company name. You need to designate folders for copies of Web job postings, ads, recruiter, and resumes and cover letters you presented in applying for the job(s).

- There are several advantages provided by phone screenings—you can take full advantage of not being face-to-face with the interviewer. You can have all the work and information spread out in front of you.

   Don't shuffle the papers while answering questions or looking for information.

- It is important to realize that your vocabulary, how questions are answered, and enthusiasm is all the telephone interviewer has to go on. Make these moments count. You may want to create a short outline of your key job skills, and core behaviors to help in your presentations. Remember to smile! When you smile your voice is clearer and you will sound much more positive and confident. One client shared with us how he stands up at home when he gets a call from an interviewer. Another mounted a mirror in front of himself so that he could look into it and pretend he was talking to a real person!

- It should go without having to say this but be sure your phone equipment is of good quality, a handset that allows you to cradle it, if using a portable phone check the batteries—stay in range and try not to use a cell phone or other device. Ensure that you have recorded a professional message (not your kids and no songs, etc.). Please folks, if you have call waiting don't answer it. You may well find that the recruiter is insulted by this and your application could end up in 'file thirteen'!

- If you are not sure of your abilities talking on the phone, get a friend to role-play with you and record your results. This will give you first-hand knowledge about how you're coming across answering the questions on the phone. Prepare — Prepare — Prepare and

Practice — Practice — Practice!

- It is important to remember something we have stated before—you are responsible for the outcome of the interview and getting your message across. The interviewer is, or should be in charge of the interview. In preparation for interviewing, it is essential that you revisit your work history and determine where and how you accomplished something in the job you held. As we have stated before, in most interviews the interviewer/ recruiter is initially interested in the last 10-15 years of work history in macro terms and very specific micro data about accomplishments in your last position. You need to determine what accomplishments in your background might be used to make the point or demonstrate that you possess certain skills, knowledge, abilities and behaviors.

- Once these are identified you then want to look at each example in order to describe what was the **situation**, what **action** did you take to resolve the situation using specific skills, and then what was the result of this activity. Remember to keep in mind, if at all possible, include **results** in some quantifiable change, e.g./ volumes added, impact to revenues, cost savings or reduced something, improving productivity, staying within budget, meeting time frame. And lastly, remember a statement of **behaviors** (SARB).

> —You are responsible for the outcome of the interview and getting your message across.

Remember that most employees are hired to do a specific job. For the use of their labor, they are paid a wage and in most cases, keep their job. How individuals get to be promoted or receive additional responsibility is to do 110% — 120% or simply get results on the assignment given. The same holds true in the interview; the company wants a person who can demonstrate those elements.

- When determining which accomplishments work to best demonstrate particular behaviors or a specific track record of results, remember that these can also be used very successfully in the construction of your resume. The typical opening question, *Tell me about your background,* is a good time for you to use selected accomplishments to make your presentation complete.

- Being knowledgeable and comfortable with your selected accomplishments will, in most cases, give you the confidence to handle the interview processes. Practice how to present them and you will worry less about what kind of questions the interviewer is going to ask. You will already be prepared. Why? Where does the material that the interviewer uses to question you come from if not taken from your resume and application?

    Additional questions are usually examples of the requirements of the company and the position. If the accomplishments you chose don't possess some form of result—a return on the investment of time, resources, and money, look further for examples. There is a simple question to ask yourself when the accomplishment is written: "What is different?"

    Example: I hired and trained 10 direct reports! "So What?" You need to elaborate on this, for instance: did you use advertisement? an agency (fee paid)? employee referral? or internal postings? What happened as a result of your training? All of these different actions have different costs for those ten hires. This exercise will put your results in perspective, quickly.

- On more than one occasion we have had clients who experienced difficulty when developing their accomplishment statements. We told them to go to the potential list of questions that an interviewer or recruiter may ask them and as they read the question, try to relate it to their own examples of work—examples that would answer the question. In most cases, it was time well spent and again enhanced the further development of their job search tools.

- On specific cases we have also recommended that the person locate someone in their network who may actually be in a similar position and ask if she would be willing to discuss the job and key skills.

- Now that you have identified the key accomplishments or developed vignettes, you must be prepared to practice them so your descriptions are concise but still get the information across.

- As we have discussed in other parts of the book, a very powerful tool that you can utilize is to have someone ask you the interview questions and have your answers video-taped. The closer you can make this exercise to the real interview, the more prepared you will be when the actual phone call comes.

- As you are developing your background information it is a perfect time to begin identifying examples of your work. This topic is also part of what we refer to as the "Briefing Book," a fact book prepared by you to take to the interview (see Chapter 8). This is even more essential if you are in the creative professions.

- Even if you are not in the creative fields you can increase your ability to tell your story; for example if you are in technology, you can show project flow charts; Marketing & Sales: select specific awards earned, new products to market graphs; Engineers: productivity improvements. Providing examples can help interviewers grasp your potential output at their organization.

- While in preparation for the interview, it is necessary to do research on what you are worth in the market. Also, by knowing your worth you can build a better search strategy insuring you are knowledgeable of what you contribute is worth X dollars in return.

- The basics can be easily obtained from Internet sites like www.salary.com, www.wageweb.com or www.salarysource.com. Also in building your search strategy, a text titled: *1500+ Key Words for $100,000+ Jobs,*

(Wendy S. Enelow, CPRW, 1998) may prove useful. There will be more information about discussing salary and negotiating a compensation package in later chapters (and developed in detail in Chapter 10).

- The next activity on your getting-prepared list should be developing a job search and marketing plan. As part of this plan each person needs to determine if he is willing to relocate for an opportunity. How is relocation going to impact the family, the working spouse or children, and does relocation increase ability to get hired or not? How large is the marketplace and companies that need these skills? For example, if you are a C.F.O. it is apparent that there is only one position per company. There are several planning aspects to consider.

Knowing Yourself *Truthfully*

Truth of Interviews is the opportunity to talk about yourself, to discuss in a sequence of interview questions what you can do and talk about what you have done.

> Has it occurred to you that you will know the majority of what could be discussed in the interview—you only have to prepare and participate.

The premise is you know yourself better than anyone else because you have looked at yourself from formative years, through working time, prior employment. You know what the job requires, have considered your behaviors for this position and have practiced your delivery. You have considered your attitude, which is very important in that a lot of interviews are lost here. We ask you, is there anyway for you not to do a good job in the interview, even if you are being interviewed by someone who doesn't know the job or isn't properly trained in interviewing? **The interview, once you are there, is your responsibility!**

Knowledge is Powerful, Right?
Don't Turn it Into Fool's Gold

You will need to create an environment where the buyer sees the same qualifications as you do (fit) and she begins to want you as an employee. Again, it goes back to the basics of interviewing—developing a relationship with the interviewer.

When you are interviewed and questioned, answer with enthusiasm. You are able to use examples from your formative years to display how you have handled similar situations. The human interest stories you have chosen from your work history will give ample opportunity to incorporate your behaviors into your answers.

If you are not interviewing every week, you should still be practicing the interview. It's just like preparing for a golf tournament or running a race, you play like you practice. Always let your actions drive the process and you won't be caught short.

Quick Interview Reference

Information/ Networking Meeting

Goal:	-Establish rapport (must understand your job) -Obtain/ share information and contacts— referrals
Challenge:	-Short time frame for meeting -May turn into interview (be ready to switch gears)
Strategy:	-Focus on your agenda and relationship building (likeability factor) -Be flexible—leave behind a positive image -Be prepared to deliver a short presentation; could receive interview-type questions

Telephone Screening/ Interview

Goal:	-To communicate key skills to get to the next step—to the interview
Challenge:	-Getting screened out over the phone—doing follow-up
Strategy:	-Deliver only enough about background to arouse curiosity -Be well prepared—organized -Use notes -Try to get the screener talking -Demonstrate a positive attitude and enthusiasm

Decision Interview

Goal:	-Pass the "behavior fit" test—reach out with a positive attitude -Show and tell of accomplishments—solve the problems
Challenge:	-Lack of interviewing experience for you (practice) -May be interviewed by someone who doesn't have a lot of experience -Interview is not focused—unable to build rapport
Strategy:	-Attempt to guide the interview—be personable—demonstrate key behaviors -Do your homework—prepare key information necessary to match your qualifications to position requirements -Be assertive if necessary, but not controlling—employ your likeability factor

Sequential/ multi-meetings

Goal:	-Gain a rapport with all players and their roles
Challenge:	-Disorganized process -Each interview has same questions -Requires endurance—focus
Strategy:	-Pace yourself—review notes—know who you are meeting -Have specific examples of accomplishments that relate to the issues (okay to use same examples with each person) -Find out the specific goals of the position -Business cards—ask for next steps—decision plan -Try to determine composite picture of opportunity -Manage interruptions—keep focused

Panel Interview

Goal:	-To make some eye contact with each member—stay cool -Keep control in answering—ask for question to be repeated if not clear -Good eye contact—confidence—friendly—smile
Challenge:	-Difficulty in establishing connection—rapport—group-friendly -Having to answer a variety of questions in a rapid delivery -Delivery of company research material—individual questions
Strategy:	-Focus—pace yourself -Maintain good eye contact when answering questions -Stop and reference questions if you keep getting rushed -Get the group to respond to you—positive attitude—smile

Meal Interviews

Goal:	-Demonstrate you can handle yourself professionally in a social setting—fit team
Challenge:	-Not able to focus with the activity -Timing of information between personal—job -What do you really think—not being yourself—not having your notes -Interruptions from servers
Strategy:	-Don't drink alcohol -Order small or simple, easy-to-eat meal -Less formal—conversational, not question-answer

The Call Comes for You to Interview

Questions to Ask Yourself:

• Have I thought through possible interview topics?

• Am I satisfied with my level of preparation and practice?

• Who is responsible for the success of the interview?

Veek © 2007

Oh no! I have to remember all this?

Chapter 8

*Courage does not always roar. Sometimes, it's the quiet voice at
the end of the day saying, "I will try again tomorrow."*
Anonymous

Briefing Book

WHEN AN APPLICANT TARGETS a company or prepares
for an interview, conducting research on the organization is
crucial. Some obvious (and important) areas to research are:
size, products, locations, officers of the company, how the
company talks about itself, and a brief market report with financials. However, in our experience, a basic knowledge of
the company is not sufficient to make a person stand out from
other applicants. You must have a really good understanding of what makes the company perform and be able to dem-

onstrate where you can potentially fit into the organization. Most individuals keep their findings in a file folder that is not clearly organized into an easy-to-use tool. We have also discovered that many clients don't effectively demonstrate their knowledge, research findings or their interest in the opportunity. Well, what can be done to change this?

I am glad you have asked that question! You can create what is referred to in this chapter as a *Briefing Book*. This concept was developed by a team of senior executives—with whom we had the privilege of working—while they were in a transition of job/ career search. The *Briefing Book* concept takes research on a company to a new level of thinking, as you meet with an interviewer from the targeted organization. Basically it entails identifying issues about the position to be interviewed for and then pinpointing how you can make an impact on the organization.

Research findings, however, are of little use until they are organized into facts and ideas that can address the company's problems and challenges—your research should have this goal in mind. Prepare a brief presentation that shows you have digested your research. Then develop a plan of action to produce a useful perspective on how you can help the organization—your presentation will enhance your job-seeking chances.

Research, read, digest and review
what you have learned.

The fundamental use of the research is to show an interviewer that you have good in-depth knowledge of the company. This knowledge can be utilized further to create a business plan to address the employer's problem(s) and help the organization.

When you first read this advice you may become overwhelmed with the potential volume and time needed. *Relax!* What we are suggesting is for this to be done for the select few companies that you have targeted as great places to work.

The second need is when the company selects you as one of the candidates for further interviewing. Often a great amount of that level of information about the company can be found on the Web site. Now remember the concept about presenting yourself with the help of FAB: your features; advantages you bring; how you can benefit the company—this can be utilized to get past the screening interviews.

A Good Lesson

Here is an example of how the basics of the *Briefing Book* helped a young office manager secure a position. She was searching for a new job because her husband was recruited for a new opportunity and at that time, there were slim pickings for interviewing. She continued contacting and through her network was referred to a privately held company.

In the initial interview by the owner, he asked her to read their Web site and a couple of other items. The interview was set one week later. During this time, she gathered all the information about the company, had her prior work experience ready and prepared questions that she wanted answered. We met prior to her interview and she said that she found a couple of misspelled words on the Web site. Great! Bring that research into the conversation.

As the interview drew to a close she was asked *what would be some of the first things you would do if you got the job?* She mentioned a few priorities and then said *I would arrange to have the misspelled words corrected on the Web site.* She said the owner almost fell out of his chair. He indicated that he had interviewed a number of candidates but no one ever mentioned the Web site! He went on to state *you must come to work for me; what kind of money are you looking for?* She said to begin she was willing to start at xyz mid-point, but based upon her research she was more inclined to be at the 75th percentile. He said he couldn't go there and she responded with *I will start now but I want to be raised to that level in six months.* He then smiled and said *I suppose you want this offer in writing, but could we make it a confirming letter?*

All good things come to those who are prepared. She had put all her research into a 3-ring binder, labeled the sections and had a copy of the Home Page on the front. At one point in the interview the owner asked to see the "fact book" (briefing book); he said that he had never interviewed a person who came as prepared.

Key Components of a Briefing Book

Business Review

The business review for interview preparation should include a profile of the company's challenges, strengths, debate of business proposition, marketing strategy, etc.

What does this tell you?

- how your job fits with the mission of the organization, corporate performance, or profitability;
- bullet-proof yourself by anticipating what they are looking for;
- what you can contribute to grow revenue, reduce costs, and streamline processes to improve company efficiency;
- is this realistic, can you hit the mark?

Presentation/ write-up:

- clear picture of the company's business, products, and competition;
- your understanding of problems and challenges the hiring manager/ employer faces;
- plan describing how you would do the work the employer needs done to address the challenges/ opportunities;
- estimate of what/ how much you could add to the bottom line/ profitability.

Assess the company's reputation:

- your network of contacts can be very valuable here;
- quality of "Key Officers";
- is this a growth opportunity or a duplicate of what you have done before?
- can you learn from them?
- attrition and is this a new position?
- what is available to review of customer opinion surveys?

You may be working with a professional search firm (headhunter) and they should be able to share everything that is known about the company so you can be fully prepared for the interview. If this information is not made available, then ask for it.

Knowledge gained from recruiter:

- information about the employer, the job, the manager and their team, and why is the job open/ opportunity available;
- should be in a position to tell you about the interview process itself, how the manager evaluates candidates, how his team will be involved in the interviews, and how the selection process will play out;
- your potential fit with the company and manager— culture;
- should be in the position to tell you about salary; and
- the company's historical performance.

Organize in concert with the potential interviewers. Practice key messages and talking points that you wish to deliver to demonstrate your understanding of the problems facing the organization, or industry, and your ability to solve or prevent them. Create a diagram/ list that matches your strengths to their needs. In addition, include an overall picture of where (flexibility/ versatility) your strengths match their deficient areas (your version of gap analysis).

Key Informational Summary

Develop a key informational summary that you could refer to if necessary. Include information such as:

- company profile
- proper name/ major corporate office/ plant locations
- Chairman/ CEO/ President/ CFO
- principle products/ services
- mergers/ acquisitions pending
- hiring manager/ title
- annual revenue
- market demographics
- projected growth
- major competitor(s)
- mission/ professional slogan
- international operations
- media releases
- any lawsuits
- call for an investor's kit or product literature
- recent downturns/ downsizing
- Standard and Poor Corporate Records
- D&B Million Dollar Database

Have we lost you yet? Seems or feels like information overload? Remember the purpose is two-fold; first, you are trying to make a decision about what organization you are going to trust your future with—with which you have a chance of success. Second, you want to WOW them as a candidate to the point they start recruiting you.

When doing research for the briefing book, create a mental map/jot down notes of what you want to explore. It's important to stay focused about what information you need. You can spend an excess of time if not careful. If you happen to have more than one interview (let's hope), budget your time. If you have to consider relocation to a different city, be prepared with Cost Of Living Averages in the new city. This is valuable if the subject of salary surfaces early in the interview process.

If caught with time constraints, at least consider looking at *Hoovers, Gale's* media information (Goliath), *Yahoo! Financial*, and if you have *Wall Street Journal* on-line, then use their briefing book option in Career Journal. These services will provide you with some good background and current information. If available, ask your financial advisor for most recent financial research notes.

The way to house this research data is to prepare a binder with dividers that will enable you to access the material quickly. You could download a copy of the company's logo from their Web site and put it into the clear insert of the cover. Take it with you to the interview and look for the opportune time to let the interviewer (especially your potential boss) know what you have prepared. She will be impressed and many times will want to review it. In your practice for the interview be sure to include the briefing book. Good luck!

Briefing Book

Questions to Ask Yourself:

- Have I identified the best prospective companies?
- Have I clearly organized and reviewed my research?
- What is my plan for show and tell?

Better practice or I'll end up with
an empty dance card!

Chapter 9

I tell you and you forget.
I show you and you remember.
I involve you and you understand
Eric Butterworth

How To Dance the Dance of The Interviewer

THE CRUCIAL STEP TO a successful interview is persuading employers that you can meet the business needs of the company and fit comfortably into a team and their culture. Most of these interactions will be one-to-one: you and a network person, recruiter or interviewer.

The phrase "Dancing with the Interviewer" is actually the name of a training session we conducted so clients can experience the variety of interviews and interviewer situations they might encounter while conducting their job search. The class was divided into tri-pods and each group consisted of an observer, interviewer, and interviewee. We prepared scripts for the interviewer to act out a specific role for the interviewee. The observer would take notes and provide feedback for both the interviewee and group. Each individual had a turn being the interviewee.

This role-play session, in concert with a personal interview practice session, was always rated the most helpful by the clients. It would be a good idea for you to emulate this activity—find yourself a knowledgeable partner who will play the interview role, someone who can view your performance critically and provide constructive feedback.

Dress for Success

We also videotaped the clients individually in a session that provided a realistic interview environment. We requested they come to this session dressed as if they were going to a company interview.

Dress for success was really tested. For instance, many folks said their interview attire wouldn't fit or it was outdated. Someone wore black shirt and white tie (ouch), there were cases of holes in the soles of their shoes (not shined), and sometimes men wore too much aftershave.

The women fared much better as many were in tune with the subject of attire for an interview. Only a few suggestions needed to be made to the women such as: too much jewelry, dangling bracelets that clanged on the table, the choice between pantsuits or business suits, scarves, and also too much perfume. One interesting client came dressed very appropriately except she had a diamond ring of about five carats on her right hand! It might appear to an interviewer she didn't need to work! It also got in the way of a good handshake.

A good rule of thumb is to remember that you are not dressing as if you were already an employee. Dress a level above the company dress code. For example, if you know that the company has a relaxed dress code of blue jeans and t-shirts, wear slacks and a button-down shirt or pantsuit—something business-like without overdressing.

The Interview Begins

To continue our realistic training session, we had the client come to the office and be greeted by the receptionist. Of course we had some role-plays designed for this exercise because we wanted the practice to be as real as possible. There were some interesting observations (even though we discussed them in our training sessions, people are creatures of habit) such as:

- arriving late for the interview;
- not being nice to the receptionist;
- displaying odd personal habits while waiting; and
- talking on the cell phone.

Sometimes we would role-play a situation in which the client was told that the interview was canceled, just to see how the issue was dealt with. Most of the time (not always, but most of the time), the client recovered and arranged a follow-up appointment.

Remember the interview starts from the time you wake up that morning (or most likely, even the night before). We have had clients tell us they had a little road rage on the way only to find this same person at the company they were interviewing with. What are the odds of that? Another client related the experience of how he got into a crowded elevator, didn't say anything to his fellow riders and then found himself sitting in front of someone who was on the elevator—how would that make you feel?

First Impressions

As we engage in this process we know that more often than not the first impression is the *buy* or the *look for reasons to turn down*; and this first impression takes place in about ten-to-fifteen seconds as the interviewer shakes your hand. Be aware of your handshake, which is part of the introduction, and reach out, go palm-to-palm firmly but not hard, two shakes and disengage.

There is the eye contact, smile and in some cases, if the handshake isn't good, try it again. Women need to be prepared for the interviewer who doesn't engage a woman's hand and only catches half the hand—reach out and try it again. If you have perspiration or wet palms, have a tissue available so you are extending a dry palm. *It matters!*

> . . . the first impression is the buy or
> the look for reasons to turn down

So, what matters in the first ten-to-fifteen seconds of the interview? The following list provides good information to be aware of:

- how you are dressed and the quality of the attire;
- your grooming (shoes shined front and back);
- do you need a haircut? is your hair style pleasing to the eye? if you have facial hair, is it neat and tidy?
- don't carry a brief case; if needed, a small purse only; buy yourself a portfolio case just large enough to hold some resumes, note pad for notes, your business cards, briefing material, and that is it;
- leave the cell phone in the car or make sure it is turned off;
- eye contact is important and listening is CRITICAL throughout the interview;
- confidence is shown by standing tall; take up some space, but don't invade the other person's space, as it will cause them to step backwards;
- practice being 'bright-eyed and bushy-tailed'!
  – show the interviewer that you are energetic and enthusiastic.

Professional recruiters have shared with us they can make nearly twenty-one evaluations in the first 10-15 minutes of meeting an applicant. So it is of vital importance that you know the dance steps and dance with the interviewer, otherwise, you are merely mimicking him or her.

The Next Dance Step

Now that you have made it through the first part of the interview, it is on to the next dance step. Determine what the interviewer is interested in learning about your background and how your skills match-up with the company's needs.

You recognize the dance as the interviewer asks you questions and begins to make moves that will provide the information in such a way that it answers his/ her needs and makes for a smooth discussion. The interviewer is impressed with your content and delivery, and then invites you back for another dance.

Often Ron and I would start an interview training session (yes, we always tried to double team) with an explanation that interviewing is truly like trying to dance with someone.

Remember back to the days in school where there was a dance and you were either very experienced or like the rest of us we had two left feet? Worse yet, you were so focused on the one dance style that you'd practiced last night that when you had your chance to dance, the band played a different tune—requiring different moves! Yikes! Remember those awful experiences?

This is a good reason for not concentrating on memorization of potential interview questions and responses.

It is worth your time to research, prepare and practice (and practice and practice!) how you will respond to different types of interview styles. Practice can help you to relax as well as reduce the fear of the unknown; it will also build your confidence. Again, if you practiced answering questions pre-determined from your research this should provide you with possibilities for different questions. You want to be able to anticipate these questions and prepare responses to them.

Thinking about what questions will be asked and how to answer them will reduce the anxiety of not knowing an answer. This is where the resume plays a role, as it is likely that you will be asked about all of the resume information.

The challenge is to practice and use all the tools in your "interview tool bag," so you can move forward with confidence in handling the sometimes-unpredictable interview situations.

Strike-up The Band, Let's Dance

You can try to prepare for every possible interview situation and spend a lot of time memorizing answers (wrong dance step) and as luck has it, when you walk into an interview there is something new happening. Ouch! The realistic approach is practice the delivery and be comfortable with the presentation of your achievements. Know what your behaviors are and tell your success stories peppered with results. Be prepared for the interview session; use the core steps listed next as guidance, and you will stay in-step with the interviewer.

Preparing for the Interview Session

1. Research the Company

Do your research on the company; learn all you can about the posted job, as well as the market position of the company. If possible, find out who the interviewer will be; this may be as simple as asking the company for an interview schedule—usually this comes from Human Resources. Practice how to answer job-related background questions, and anticipate what they may ask about accomplishments listed on your resume. You want to have stellar answers for every question or requirement and if you anticipate the question, you can practice how to handle them with ease.

2. Review Interview Approaches

Review the various interview approaches. Today, and most likely into the next decade, the number one interview approach in most companies will be the situational or behavioral-based interview. The interviewer wants examples of past performances that show you are able to handle specific situations. Each question has a behavior as its subject matter—listen for it and answer with a SARB that focuses on demonstrating that behavior. It has been our experience that in most interviews the questions you are asked will relate exactly to what they are looking for in the position.

3. Interview Environments

Understand the different type of interview environments such as a panel, group, phone, or meal (*see Chapter 7*). If managing people is part of the job, often your potential staff will be allotted time to meet with you and ask you some questions. Don't allow the time to be consumed by your answers; ask them to answer some of your questions. Get them talking and try to get them to describe what they would want from the person who will be their boss. Some other possibilities are:

- in their opinion, what are some of the priorities?
- how long have they worked for the company?
- if the situation is right, ask them what would they like to do more of or what career goals they have?
- ask about expectations during the first few days on the job.

4. Review Sample Interviews

If you have access, you can listen to audiotapes or view sample interview videos. It is well worth the effort to get someone to ask you the questions and videotape your answers. In learning anything new you need to prepare – prepare – prepare and practice – practice – practice. This will help prepare a positive mindset and be more comfortable when the actual interview time arrives.

5. Organize Your Main Points

Determine what accomplishments in your background can be used to demonstrate that you *do* possess the necessary behaviors and job knowledge. It is a good idea to use a 3 x 5 card or a strip of paper and make an outline of specific background behaviors and job knowledge; you could refer to this, if needed, during the interview.

Be creative (this is why we recommend an interview portfolio so you can have these notes, extra resumes, as well as a pad of paper to take notes)!

Remember to provide concise answers to the interview questions . . . and then stop talking. If you ramble on you could inadvertently state something unintended. There is a lot of power in silence.

6. Prepare Your Own Questions

Prepare your questions about the company ahead of time. Even if you find that your questions have been answered in the interview meetings, make the statement: *most of my questions* [pause] *were addressed, such as* . . . (list several areas that you were going to probe).

It's better than saying *I don't have any!* This could be misinterpreted by the interviewer; he or she may assume that you are not interested. Resist the temptation to ask questions related to benefits, money, and hours! These should and will be addressed at the time of the offer.

7. Know When the Interview Starts

When contact is made with the company or you are asked to call in to make the arrangements for the interview, *the Interview Has Started*. Begin using your chemistry-building with the staff. When you arrive at the location, make sure the front office staff is greeted professionally. In most cases, the lead interviewer or manager will ask them their opinion.

8. Envision the Entire Process

Start envisioning the whole strategy of interviewing by thinking through not only the interviews, but, all the potential events that might happen between the first meeting and getting an offer. Have a goal or goals for each step. As simple as it sounds be ready to answer a question like, *what order would you prefer to be in for the interviewing?* The last person in an interview, percentage wise, is more successful versus the earlier applicants.

Now we all can't dictate the order, so we need tactics planned to stand out in the hiring authority's mind regardless of the pecking order. For example: if you are first of several people to interview, the process of meeting all the applicants could take several weeks. It may be hard for the interviewer to remember you. So during the waiting time you should keep some form of contact with the interviewer. It can be a simple e-mail stating that you are still interested, along with mention of a point from the interview, or something new if you feel it would capture interest. The opposite is true for the last person to be interviewed. The turn around for a decision can happen fast so you will want a plan for responding quickly with a thank-you note.

9. Honesty

I think we should put glowing lights around these next two points. As we performed post-interviews with clients we asked what part of the interview would they most like to have a second chance at; we heard two responses over and over again.

The first advice: if you don't know the answer to a question, be honest and say so.

The second: when asked a question of a situation that you actually did not experience, say, *I can't recall that I have ever been in that situation, but if I was, this is how I would respond* or *this is what I would do. . .* You will receive some credit for the answer.

10. Answer the Question. Period

After you answer the question remember to stop talking. If you are in a behavioral-based interview the question usually starts out with these words, *tell me about a time . . .* or *give us an example of . . .* Take your time to organize your response before speaking. Don't elaborate or ramble. And remember, your answer should be about 1.5–2 minutes in length.

Common and Difficult Questions to Consider

Sometimes what appears to be a basic interview question can actually turn into the most potentially difficult to answer. You have made it through the screening and are now engaging in information gathering for yourself. At the same time, you are also presenting a picture of yourself that attracts the employer—makes him want to learn more about you. The interviewer (*in most cases*) is not out to trick you or confuse the situation by asking meaningless questions.

Again, early into the interview you will be able to determine the questioning approach so you can feel confident that the dancing steps you have practiced are recognized. Remember, however, that the value of practicing with thought-out questions is to focus on yourself and your relationship to a potential position within the company.

Recruiters and interviewers have told us that they often reach a decision early in the interview as to how much time they plan spending with an applicant. Most folks can sense this, so take a deep breath and adjust to the circumstances (a new dance). The questions listed on the next page are what we describe as "taking the lid off" or "getting started" —to see where the interviewer may be headed.

> We never get a second chance to
> make a good first impression.

If you are fortunate and the interviewer is well trained, she will take a couple of minutes to explain what will take place or happen in the interview. There is no substitute for your own common sense in determining how best to respond to an actual interview question (This is why we suggest practicing the potential interview questions!).

We never get a second chance to make a good first impression. For both men and women, make a small investment and buy a portfolio for interviewing (leave your office at home!). The more items you carry the greater the chance for something to go wrong.

Sample Questions:

Tell me about yourself: Any applicant who stumbles over this question usually raises a red flag in the interviewer's mind that here is a person who may not be prepared. This is the best place to use your 1-2-minute presentation. There is no hard and fast rule but you may want to try these suggestions and cover the four areas:

(1) overview of work background;

(2) mention two key accomplishments that relate to the position;

(3) mention education and special training; and your current situation.

Why are you available? Unless your answer raises concern by the interviewer, there is nothing to worry about. Just don't dwell on the details. For sure don't convey baggage such as anger or bitterness and don't be embarrassed if you were terminated, downsized, laid-off.

Now if you were released for cause (poor performance, etc.) you should take some extra time to rehearse your answers so that you are comfortable with follow-up questions. Everyone deserves a second chance; this is where references can play a big difference.

What were your most significant contributions in your former position? Make sure your answer relates to this new position; keep it brief. Let the interviewer ask for details. Doing your homework will help you to have a good example(s).

Make a short list that you can refer to. If you have done your homework on the company you will be able to reference the key accomplishments you have worked out and connect them to the job requirements.

Express your contributions in the SARB format.

What do you know about our company? This is a gift for you—open up your briefing book, which contains the research you have done on the company and maybe includes a copy of the company's home page. Believe us, it will impress the interviewer. Then answer the question (refer to *Chapter 8* for developing a briefing book).

In what ways do you feel qualified for this position? This is your open door, don't be shy or hesitate. Remember all the accomplishments you listed. Frame your answer so that it relates to the organization's needs. If the interviewer referenced information about the job, include it as you reply. Use your behaviors to set yourself apart from other candidates. Get your message across.

How would your former manager describe your performance? If it was good, then go with it! If it was a less-than-ideal working situation, don't disguise the facts; just build on the results. Maybe you and your manager didn't always agree, but that never got in the way of doing a good job. If you have a letter of recommendation, this is one of those times to bring it out. The question is designed to bring out what kind of employee you are as referenced by someone else.

What is one skill that you would like to improve? Now don't go global or say you don't have one, and don't nail yourself either. Respond with a behavior that, if worked too hard, can be a weakness. As an example, *When I push to get a job done sometimes I can get very focused, causing me to be overzealous and too demanding of my team. I am very aware of this so I have learned to catch myself, pull back and check in with the progress of the team.*
   It is not enough to tell the interviewer of a skill that needs improving. Give a specific example and tell steps taken to improve.

What level of salary have you earned? What are your salary needs? In both cases, don't just blurt out a figure. You don't want to eliminate your candidacy early. The interviewer needs information to ensure he can afford you. Try to meet him halfway by saying: *Based upon my research and other interviews, jobs at this level pay in the range of X to X*, giving a range gap of 20%.

Then ask, *What is the range of the position we are discussing?* and/or *Where do I fall in the range of the position we are discussing?*

Make Sure You Are In Rhythm

We chose to stop here to transition from "Setting-the-Stage Questions" to more information about the interview process and setting. There are additional questions to review in *Coaches Corner* V that represent a cross section of questions typically asked by interviewers.

Again, as we have discussed, you do not want to gamble and try to memorize responses to certain questions. In practicing the interview, build on your selected accomplishments and know your behaviors so that you can deliver your accomplishment examples. Think "SARB" to help formulate responses. That way it doesn't matter what the questions being asked are, you will be equipped to answer them.

Remember that nearly all the information being sought by the interviewer will come from your background and experiences.

> No one knows you better
> than you, right?

Mirror the style and techniques of your interviewer. Listen with all your senses, from the moment you leave for the interview and you enter the property to the time you leave the property. It's not over yet because while the information is fresh in your mind, it is time to debrief. As your interview schedule unfolds, pay attention to everything said including the small talk. The list below contains example questions to ask yourself after the interview:

- Did I answer forthrightly?
- Did I come across credible?
- Did I stop after answering a question or did I over elaborate?
- Did I ramble?
- Did I draw a blank for a question? If so, how did I respond?
- Did I ask for clarification if something was not clear?

- Did I smile?
- Did I notice silences, facial expressions, gestures, body language, etc. that could be meaningful? In which parts of the interview did this occur?
- Did the interviewer especially react to something I said?
- Was I effectively highlight my distinguishing characteristics—behaviors?

At times an applicant may be so excited that they get started with the interview before the interviewer. Wait and let the interviewer lead. Enthusiasm can be a key tool you want to employ. It shows you have the can-do spirit. Aggressive eagerness is often not perceived as a positive trait. It can project aloofness and this usually backfires.

Whether your interview is with one person or several, take the time to get names and exact titles. Our recommendation is that applicants take the time to have business cards made up to represent at least your name and contact information. Then in the exchange of cards no one is left out and often the interviewer is impressed that you have developed a business card.

Also as you network the
business card is a tool
that helps you stand out.

Make sure you get cards as you begin to schedule networking meetings. Take them to the interview and give them to everyone you come into contact with. It makes a great impression in how thorough you are, but most important, it helps them remember you.

As the allotted time draws down try to get a commitment for a follow-up meeting or visit to the work area. Probe to see if additional people need to see you. Don't sound desperate, just interested. Ask: *What are the next steps?*

There are countless situations and experiences you will run into and there isn't just one set of guidelines to use nor is there a specific behavior that will be right for every situation.

Remember that acceptance usually starts with identifying the wants of the buyer (interviewer). If you can get the interviewer talking about the company, the position and the problems facing that area, this will really help you when it's your turn to deliver why you meet the company's needs.

As an applicant, you are not only in the meeting to be asked questions but as we have said before, you also need to have your questions answered. At a minimum you need to find out about the job, company, boss and culture. Ask the interviewer what types of behaviors would best suit the position.

Remember a job decision (hiring and acceptance) is a mutual commitment. When things are being wrapped-up you may get a direct response to how things went by getting invited back. If that is not the case, get some commitment as to when you can follow-up for the next steps. State that you are (if you are) very interested and would like the opportunity to discuss the position further.

Do a post analysis about what you think and need to do further. Send or hand-deliver a thank-you note; either handwritten if your handwriting is good or type it and sign it. You could also email a thank-you note, but this is much less personal and won't stand out in the interviewer's mind to the same extent.

Put a date in your day-timer for follow-up. Make a list of things that you might do to keep your name in front of the company. Review your network contacts to see if you remember anyone who knows this company. They could help your candidacy. Lastly, bring your references and/ or your job search team up to date.

The three key things to remember for interviewing are:
prepare; prepare; prepare; and practice;
practice; practice . . . and smile. Okay that's seven!

Remember to review the total list of questions found in *Coaches Corner* V and develop your natural response to them. Then practice (it will cure the sweaty palms!).

How to Dance the Dance of the Interviewer

Questions to Ask Yourself:

• Do I know my best dance approach?

• Is my dress appropriate for an interview? have I checked myself in the mirror?

• Am I in tune with what makes me unique and standout from the competitors?

Negotiations can be a win-win situation if you
start from a position of knowledge.

Chapter 10

*The more we learn to operate in the world of trust
in our intuition, the stronger our channel will be
and the more money we will have.*
Shakti Gawain

Negotiation Principles and Guidelines

WELCOME TO THE BEST part of a job search campaign. If
you are re-reading this chapter you have either received an
offer or you are anticipating one. Congratulations!

A frequent question from clients is: *when do we start the
negotiations?* The answer in broad terms is that some form of
negotiation begins at the start of the job interview and usually ends with the offer or a compensation package being presented. When we refer to *negotiations*, it's normally for discus-

sion dealing with the salary offer or sometimes a hire package. Benefits, vacation time, and other topics are part of the starting package, but salary is key in setting the stage for the discussion of the other areas.

Who Handles Negotiations

So when do you start the negotiations? It has been our experience that *when* will depend, in many cases, on the company's style and also, it will often depend on the size of the company.

In the smaller organizations (sometimes privately owned) the principal will want to set the salary or at least be involved. In a larger company, salary negotiations will usually fall to the human resources (HR) department with the involvement of an executive with profit/ loss responsibility.

If the future position is chief executive officer (CEO), a senior member of the board of directors and the head of HR will deliver the message. As a new chief operating officer (COO) position, most likely the CEO will be the closer or welcome you, but the HR department will often deliver the initial conditions for employment.

At the staff level, often the hiring manager will make the offer, followed by HR to cover benefits, etc. If there is a contract or complicated job performance criteria, this can involve stock, bonuses or perks; an attorney may participate in the process. Often at the senior level where a contract is to be signed, an applicant will have his/her own legal guidance.

There may be a third party (agency or retained recruiter) handling the negotiations. If it is an *agency*, there is roughly a 50/50 chance that they will deliver the offer. If there is a search firm involved, their *retained recruiter* is the messenger about 95% of the time. Again, if the hiring manager has the budget responsibility for your salary, he will be involved with HR and often with you directly.

Some advice: if you have an agency (who is on commission) handling the negotiations, make sure they keep you apprised of the negotiations. The agency may be trying to get a higher salary in order to increase their commission and not be concerned with your future in that company. You may be willing to take a lesser salary and receive other concessions. Knowing your limits is extremely important as well as knowing what you're willing to give up for an opportunity.

Job Responsibility Negotiations

Before you can begin any *negotiations of a job offer*, you have to get the offer! Right? This is not always the case when you are dealing with the *job responsibility negotiations*—negotiations that involve the interviewee's skills in relation to the job description; there may be a willingness to add to the job and thus make it more valuable.

The real key to remember as you become the final candidate is to be prepared. You need to be armed with job responsibility information, research data on the company, and salary level information; as well, know what you want to achieve and where you are willing to flex/ compromise.

Remember the company usually wants to hire a person at the minimum up to the mid-point of the salary range. So, if you are very experienced and have already moved your salary into perhaps the 75th percentile of the job range, you will need a plan to get the offer increased or have other concessions to consider. If you feel that you bring more experience to the job, it will take a plan to demonstrate your worth.

There are Web sites that can provide you with salary ranges for most positions in a company. They are quite easy to find and research. We will discuss the negotiation process further in the *Coaches Corner* (Section XII) so you will have a good working knowledge/ understanding.

Remember: There is a job for
everyone; all we have to do is find it.

In many cases negotiation is a testing or probing process of individuals investigating each other's needs and then agreeing upon some solutions to meet each party's wants/ values. The solutions should be within the affordability of the individual and to the satisfaction of the hiring authority. The company paying the wage usually wants some form of guarantee for the investment and wants a return that will contribute to a goal, standard, result or increase in revenues. The company has therefore placed a value on the work they expect to be performed—this was discussed in the previous chapter and is known as *job ranges*.

You may have done market research, found salary levels for your job and already have set a certain salary level. You may have also determined, that because you possess the knowledge/ track record, years of experiences, education and training, and behaviors, you are expecting a specific market level salary. If there is a major gap between the two, then it can mean that either you or the company may have unrealistic expectations around the discussion about value added or degree of difficulty for performing the job.

Okay, now what? The company is saying, *we really need this person, but how can we afford her*? The applicant is saying, *I really want that job; what am I willing to do*? In the scheme of negotiations, if the individual feels the company did not treat her with fairness, the position may be accepted but without a 100% commitment. It can remain a sore point as you attempt to do your job. This situation may even keep you active in the job market. There are working situations where a person has been in a job for quite sometime and has maxed out the salary range. Because of the competitiveness of the job market for a position (which is ever-changing), another possibility can occur: a person can appear over-paid for the duties they perform.

There are two basic elements to negotiation:
•Job responsibilities
•Salary investment

Most applicants want to advance themselves and will interview for a higher-level job. In those situations the minimum to mid-point of the salary range should work. If the company hires you at a higher salary level than the current employees doing the same job, it can create a variety of potential problems: a possible compression issue for HR to manage; a potential relationship target for the recipient and his peers; or, performance expectations where it is unrealistic of the company to get a return.

Oh boy, what a bunch of "ifs" to manage. If it were possible to track this situation you would most likely find a multitude of endings. The process for negotiation of management and/or executive positions takes on differences about what is open for discussion, but the basics remain the same.

Remember there are two basic elements that should be accomplished, first that the job responsibilities are understood—what is expected of you to perform in the job and how you are to be measured to determine your effectiveness. The second element is the salary investment, once a decision to hire is made. Take comfort in the fact that usually if the negotiations are a win-win process for both parties, the final decision will be beneficial to both parties. Therefore, to create a win-win, the research about a position's value compared to what you have been making is an absolute must.

Salary Negotiations

Often in staff level positions the salary levels are pretty well fixed and not subject to negotiations. If you bring a skill that is not part of the job description, you may be able to get the employer to agree to a higher salary. If this doesn't work, read on. If you recall earlier in our book, we stated that salary levels often are based upon market supply of qualified applicants— they may also reflect the value of the position in the industry/ market (not all industries or companies pay the same for the same position).

Remember that each position has a value and a contribution factor built into the grade of the position. The value of a job is related to the degree of difficulty of duties; the value of the job in an organization and the value of the position within the industry is impacted by availability.

Market value can be driven down if there is a flooding of similar positions in the market and/or an abundance of qualified applicants. The most recent published example of this occurred in information technology (IT) where the profession experienced high downsizing; the market could not absorb this level of change. The companies, in a lot of cases, placed IT work on a lesser priority, out-sourced the business, and some companies actually stopped the technical projects in the works. The recovery has been long and actually is still in process as we write this book.

The point here is what is offered for IT positions, on the average, is less than what was offered a couple of years earlier; the offers also come with a different arrangement of responsibilities. The applicants had to make concessions or negotiate a different level to stay even with what they had earned before.

Just reverse the process when the market place has fewer applicants with needed skills in an industry. The medical field is a good example of increasing market value. Most medical positions and personnel are in the driver's seat and this will most likely continue to be the case for some time.

If the financial offer part is less that what you have been earning, look at the total package and see if there are other benefits that you didn't have previously. Some possibilities to consider are:

- the cost of benefits
- higher matching of the 401K, other investment opportunities
- additional vacation time
- continued training opportunities
- advancement potential
- stock options

In a review of why a candidate picked one offer over another, it was often because the company was flexible in awarding additional vacation time, which is also considered income. Now we have to burst the bubble for you. Trying to secure additional vacation time may not be possible because of company policy. Usually you will find that the bigger the company, the more rigid the salary levels and benefits; however, the upper levels' personnel have more flexibility.

If there are no benefit differences and the financial offer is less that what you have been making, evaluate the level and amount of responsibility you have in the new company — determine what they expect of this position.

We have always recommended that the applicant analyze the differences between the new job and the previous position; look for specific values, results, and goals that you can relate your experiences to, as compared to what they want. If it is less, then consider an addition to your negotiation strategy — securing more responsibility (if your experiences warrant) i.e. a different job grade therefore higher pay. Also be aware of another complicating situation. Some individuals may have received merit increases over several years in their current position, without additional responsibility and they end up being actually over-paid for the position. We have worked with folks who have reached their maximum pay grade level and only received company annual average salary increases, or nothing at all.

Be flexible with salary demands if this is your situation. There have been clients that we worked with where the job was exactly what they wanted but the salary was less than expected. Sometimes it is a good move to accept the position and once in, your performance can change things.

Willingness for relocation can
relate to market value . . .

Willingness for relocation can relate to market value and is another issue worth drawing to your attention. As you look at the population and measure the work force in age, skills and community involvement, etc. you will see an increasing number of folks who do not want to relocate. They realize it can reduce their market for job opportunities but as more families become two working professionals, often the family cannot look at relocation due to the potential financial loss if their spouse stops working.

The good news is that on the other side of the coin, a person can be in a better position if they are willing to relocate to where the jobs are. It is also an aggressive way to accelerate your career opportunities in many cases.

At this point of writing we have only touched on the two primary areas for negotiating, first being the job and second being compensation for doing the job. Our intention was to clear up some of the more common gray areas and provide you with enough information on additional topics so that you can research them. We believe that it isn't a case of one-size that fits-all when it comes to the negotiation of starting salaries. The important thing is to know your value and *to ask*; once you get to the offer stage, it is very rare that the offer is pulled back because the question was asked—of course, this depends on how it is asked—the attitude exhibited by the interviewee.

Every candidate for a potential job that has received a financial offer has to apply their own set of circumstances to their negotiation strategy.

We also have decided that the topic of executive pay is a level and discussion unto itself. We are referring those individuals to a reference book (there are many) that deals with employment agreements, conditions of employment, contracts, options, deferred income and much more. The book we've used with great success is *Perks and Parachutes* (1997) written by John Tarrant with Paul Fargis. You will find it very helpful as we have.

Depending on the level of the position within the organization, negotiations can start in the earliest stage of the job interviewing process—remember as well, that you are setting the stage for negotiations the moment you arrive at the interview. The hiring authority and company can benefit from the applicant's experiences; the same is true for the applicant in finding their values and job preferences being met in the potential position.

> . . . you are setting the stage for negotiations
> the moment you arrive at the interview.

If you are being represented by a recruiter, one of their responsibilities is to provide the employer with salary information and recommendations that will convince you to accept. Sometimes, especially in the case of agency involvement, the company has told the recruiter that they only want to see the candidate who fits into a specific salary level.

Throughout the interviewing process both sides have something at stake and the best ending is a win-win agreement for both parties. This requires open, reasonable, and honest conversations as well as equitable flexibility, without making assumptions about what the other party is thinking. We have always advised clients that a good course of action is to withhold, as long as possible, their compensation expectation, and to refer to *ranges* of salary. The best time starts when you go from being an applicant to someone they see potentially doing the job. Bottom line is: use your FAB and create your value! Let's discuss some of these buying signals.

Buying Signals

- you are still interviewing and the conversation gets very specific, references are asked for, and interviews are taking more time;

- you are progressing through the second, third interviews and are meeting with the potential manager;

- you may be asked to meet with peers (as mentioned previously when discussing interviews);

- for marketing and advertising folks, a presentation may be asked of you;

- you have passed their testing program and with some positions you may be asked to meet with an outside psychologist;

- a big green light is when the people you are interviewing with start to sell you on the company. If the position requires relocation, they invite you to consider the costs, housing, and if with a family, get them involved with house hunting trips;

- the HR department or your potential manager starts getting specific about what it will take to close the deal. Salary, fringes, performance bonuses, benefits, (relocation) assignments, physicals, and drug testing may be mentioned.

The negotiation strategy (and it's difficult) is to avoid a detailed salary discussion until you have the offer—old rule of thumb: whoever speaks first loses negotiation leverage. If salary issues arise, avoid the first pass, but if the company persists, ask what they have in mind.

Make sure the actual offer is real. It usually comes first as a verbal offer like, *We have been very impressed with your background and in our opinion we can see you doing (xyz) position for us. The salary for that position is $—.* You will hear or learn of this advice from a number of resources. Often the hiring authority will make the offer and may close with something like:

> *We want you to consider our offer completely; why not take the next week to think it through and then call us on such and such date.*

> Wow! Make some kind of commitment at this time, like: *I am very pleased with the offer and I can't think of any reason now that would cause me concern.*

If the company wants an immediate decision or one by the next morning, your response could be:

> *I am very pleased with the offer, but I want to discuss it with my family. I can get back to you by* ___ (3-5 working days is reasonable); *again, I am very appreciative about being selected and I do believe that I can meet or exceed the objectives we discussed.*

What if the offer is less than you expected? Again, keep the door open and say something like:

> *I am very pleased that you have selected me for the position; I would like a couple of days to review everything we discussed and. . . . When can I get back to you?*

Making an Informed Decision

Now before riding off into the sunset, make sure you have all the information to make that decision. At the minimum you want sufficient information regarding:

- the position,

- organizational level,
- job responsibilities,
- decision-making level,
- goals and performance expectations,
- method of performance measurement,
- rewards, and
- career advancement potentials.

Clear the process for follow-up if you have more questions. At best, we hope you have done research on the company and also have a good idea of their current market situation, competitive position and future plans.

Once the job is pretty clear, next determine a total compensation package and offer you will be comfortable with. What is the least you will accept for the position? It's not just the salary that must be considered; items such as perks (vacation time), benefits, the company's criteria for bonuses (if any), any special arrangements that a senior job level requires, and salary reviews are all important factors to take into consideration.

This type of negotiation usually results in establishing meaningful performance expectations and rewards in assuming the position. This is always a good practice for all applicants to exercise in the job search process. In the end, employment discussions hopefully mark the beginning of a long-term and mutually beneficial relationship.

Finally, you must consider the resources available to accomplish the objectives that were laid out for you. Again, if you have to relocate for the opportunity, make sure the company policy is clear as to what is covered in your move.

At the more senior levels it is not uncommon to be discussing a specific contract for employment. You will want to get the offer in writing. At this stage there may be some rub, as the company only wants to confirm your acceptance to an offer. If you have a good reason to present they may come around. Ask:

When can I take a look at the offer in writing? It will be helpful in understanding all the details of the offer and my new job.

Employment Agreement

The basic elements of an employment agreement are:

Term	how long the contract runs
Responsibility	description of the job and status
Compensation	salary, bonus, stock options; other monetary perks
Benefits	life, health insurance; retirement qualification
Severance	amount to be paid when discharged

Beyond these basics, agreements may cover other items like: car, laptop, hiring bonus, professional memberships, and conflict resolution process. Parachutes/ severances can be requested, but today more companies are moving away from this benefit. Included often in offers are non-compete and nondisclosure clauses. Lastly, consider a termination agreement (especially if you are relocating) or what the company has done in the past when downsizing or reducing positions (a change in ownership).

If you are fortunate to have more than one potential offer, buying time for a decision date from a company who has made you an offer is a delicate situation at best. You can test their willingness and focus your assessment of this decision as a major career move, not just money. Try to make them comfortable with the circumstances by saying that you really appreciate their offer, but when you started the process of career change you promised yourself that you were going to make an informed decision for your next position and carefully consider the career move. Remember there is a fine line between greed and common sense. No one wants to feel they are a second choice and sometimes if the company senses a person is hedging, they will retract their offer!

In our experience, the clients who did their homework in the beginning and knew what they wanted were prepared when the company came through with a reasonable offer; they made the decision without trying to collect another offer. The client knew where they could excel. If there were questions with the company when you began your search, this is the time to continue getting answers to your concerns, or stop. This is a simple step in reality; remember an old saying; *if it walks like a bad deal, talks like a bad deal, it usually is a bad deal.*

. . . there is a fine line between greed
and common sense

It's inadvisable however, to romance a company if you are not seriously considering them. No company wants to be the pawn in a bidding war; if they learn of this situation, they will likely resent the manipulation. What goes around comes around, folks. Occasionally it does happen; some clients we worked with have received multiple offers—this is the time to be strategic and certainly weigh all the factors so you are making an informed decision instead of an emotional one.

Most organizations are run by real people and will work with you. It shouldn't always be money that gets your vote. Quality of life, reputation of the company, passion for your work, contributions to an organization, benefits, pensions, 401ks and matching funds, career movement—a number of items should be considered.

There are benefits such as continued education, seminars to advance your technical knowledge and depending on the position, it can mean an office in the home, car allowance, computers and cell phones, to mention a few. You must think realistically—how many compromises do you have to make and will this be palatable and healthy for you over time?

A Hard Lesson

We now offer a short story to illustrate the importance of making an unemotional and informed decision. One morning, a close friend and fellow consultant came into the office to say he had accepted another consulting opportunity—for double his salary and mega bonuses. We talked—actually he did the talking and I listened—after a few minutes it became evident he had dollar signs in his eyes and the offer was feeding his ego, not his common sense.

Here was a professional who teaches the material to help others, but he wasn't applying the principles to himself. Granted, the money and potential bonuses were very attractive. As a friend I tried to interject some questions such as: what has he considered in the consulting assignments; how many compromises was he making; did he get an employment agreement or contract for at least twelve months. The answers were: no, I can handle the change, and no contract, respectively.

Well, he left and during the next three months we talked some, but he also had to travel a lot so it was hard to connect. Then I got this call one early morning to ask if we could we meet for coffee. *Sure*, I said, *is there something wrong*? His response: *I will bring you up to date when we meet*. You probably guessed it; he did lose the job, no severance, and no reference.

That morning he reflected a lot, of course, but he said *do you remember the last thing you said to me as I left your office that day*? He went on to remind me: *you told me that I have to work a full year to earn the new money, think about the compromises (changes) I have to make, and the fact that I don't have a contract, so keep this in mind as I go to accept. The knowledge and value I was bringing to that company should mean that the contract is an automatic*. I responded by saying that was what he taught me. Then I said I should have sent him a bill for the consulting advice.

Hard lessons but we learn them at some time. He landed on his feet and was again in his passion. He died two years ago, unfortunately, and I miss my friend, but he had given so much to me that his spirit is always with me. Thanks for reading the lessons he left for us.

Further Discussion

Now let's look at those situations where you are being asked to make a decision without all the necessary data. You need to bring this to the attention of the company and advise what you need to reach a decision. Sometimes it could be more time meeting the people with whom you will be working. It may be more clarity with your immediate manager as to your goals. The least amount of time is twenty-four to forty-eight hours just to review the opportunity.

How many times can you revisit an offer? We recommend twice; get it right. If you need to negotiate for money always present it last and from what values (use a FAB discussion) you bring to the position in potential added results (have examples). Don't say *I need this amount* or *in my last position I earned*; it won't fly.

Have a strategy worked out where you can set the stage by reviewing the areas that you do agree with and are willing to accept. Talk about the job needs and match those with your value, skills, and worth—the benefits you bring to the company. If they are recommending the mid-point of the salary range, you can discuss the additional experience that you bring and that you see this falling into the higher end of the range. Most managers or HR folks will respond to this kind of logic.

Sometimes by breaking the money down to a lesser amount it will come across better. For example: you want $60,000 and they are stuck on $54,000. You can say, *actually, all I am asking for is to bring me up only $500.00 per month more ($6,000 divided by 12 months)*.

In putting it all together, have a strategy, do your research, keep it at a win-win level, agree with the items that are okay and then say something like: *I have three areas to discuss: base salary, benefit coverage, and the time frame for the goals to be accomplished*. Be sensitive to the other person's reactions and note signals of acceptance. Lastly, remember the company doesn't want to have to start searching all over again for the hire or they may not be too pleased with a second choice and by now they can see you doing the job! Good hunting.

Early Negotiation Questions

The following are some questions you may come across early in the interview stages:

- if money wasn't a consideration, what would you want to do?
- what do you hope to earn three to five years from now?
- what do you feel you are worth?
- what salary do you need to support your lifestyle?
- what salary will it take to get you to work for us?
- what were you making at your last job?
- what is your salary history?
- what would be an adequate reward for your efforts?

Some Basic Cautions to Consider:

—when the offer is not what you anticipated

- be careful not to project your feelings or change your attitude. It could cause the employer to be concerned;
- if you are working with a recruiter, don't bad mouth the company to them. They may interpret this to mean you aren't interested;
- review the job and compare it to your experience, then prepare for your negotiation discussion something like:

    I am very interested in the position but please share with me how you arrived at the compensation level—did you take into consideration all of the experience that I bring and my fit for the position?

- you may be able to negotiate an early review;
- did they consider your salary history?

Be ready to deal with the responses to these questions so you are fully prepared from start to finish!

Negotiation Principles and Guidelines

Questions to Ask Yourself:

- Do I know my financial value and my needs?
- Do I have a grip on each part of the negotiation?
- Do I have a plan that will cause the company to maintain their interest in me?

Some Final Thoughts

In three words I can sum up
Everything I've learned in life:
It goes on.
Robert Frost

WE FEEL CERTAIN THAT you have learned or discovered much from reading this book and, that you are confident to interview and stand out from the other applicants. If you apply the basic principles contained in this book, you will be very well equipped to win the job offers.

We have observed many clients when beginning to experience career success. The success was achieved through learning and knowing themselves well and by applying the basic concepts we discussed.

As we presented the concepts in this book, it was our intention not to lead you on with the idea that there was a magic pill to solve all the issues. That pill doesn't exist. The process of determining behaviors may well be a first for many people—in fact, it may be the first time they have understood themselves in the working environment.

Some of the material may not be revolutionary but it contains simple proven principles to use. Many of our clients shared that not only did the interviewing knowledge help the job search but it also improved their social/ family relationships—for once, they felt that they could communicate.

As you work your way through the book or when you get that job offer and you feel that others could benefit from your experiences or there is something about interviewing you would like more insight on, please feel free to e-mail us at **ajobdoctor@aol.com** or **pawpaw2@cox.net**. If we use your idea or suggestion in our next book, we will reference you as the contributor and we will send you a free copy of the book.

Take a few minutes and let us hear from you. It's how great networks are built.

May you experience nothing but successes in your quest.
Recognize that you have the courage within you to fulfill the purpose of your birth. Summon forth the power of your inner courage and live the life of your dreams.

Gurumayi Chidvilasananda

COACHES CORNER

Ronald Venckus

David Endress

Job Doc,
I believe we've given
all our interview secrets.

Yes, we have.
Now I want to provide
some solid coaching
advice.

COACHES CORNER I

A Sensitive Area To Deal With Is:
"Why Didn't I Get the Job?"

ALMOST ALL OF US, in some form, have not received something we thought we really deserved, right? This is also true in the world of job search and career management. In the case of interviewing we have counseled clients extensively about why they didn't get the job even when they felt they were qualified and really wanted the opportunity. This is especially hard to accept when a person feels they were stellar in the interview process. It is still a good idea to review what took place in the meetings to find out if anything can be improved or isolate what could have gone wrong—whether this is:

- omitted something in the interview;
- the references didn't support the story;
- didn't sell oneself; perhaps didn't know oneself;
- research wasn't complete
- too nervous

—the CAUSE AND EFFECT GOES ON. After this step is done it may still appear you were stellar. CLOSE THE DOOR AND MOVE ON.

First and foremost, we recommend that where there is one opportunity there will be more; shake it off. Step back and review what took place in the interview process. Often there will be little signs of subtle mistakes that can be corrected with practice. For instance,

- I know I could have shown more confidence;
- I need to deliver my accomplishments and behaviors more effectively;
- I can practice my listening skills and make sure I understand what they are asking me;
- I need to do more research on the company before the interview;
- I need to develop my FAB to make a stronger impact.

Sometimes it just happens that your interview was scheduled on a day that something awful happened in the company that had everyone on edge and you ended up dealing with interviewers who were only half attentive.

It's hard to understand as well as to accept, but sometimes the fit or mismatch of personalities is the reason for turndown. The culture just wasn't a match.

A person may think it was a slam-dunk of an interview process and is over-confident that the offer is in the mail. When the turndown letter arrives instead, first there is usually some anger, denial next and the, *I didn't want to work for that company anyway!* You think: *I will call the company and find out what went wrong and get their opinion as to what can I do to improve.*

First, you probably aren't going to get through because the company has already moved on with another issue. Second, if you did get the HR person on the phone, they are NOT going to libel themselves by giving you a short feedback session or performance review. For sure, if there was another person who sold themselves more effectively, distinguished themselves better, had more experience and yes, in the real world (even if it's against the law), people will make conscious choices that aren't fair. In the latter case, they probably did you a favor by not hiring you because most people want to work for employers who would treat them fairly regardless of their circumstances.

There have been several occasions where the company

had two very qualified candidates and one was represented by an agency. Again, with all skills being the same between the candidates, the company picked the one without a fee. Sometimes it is nothing more that just being in the wrong place at the wrong time; move on, as you will never know this for sure.

Revisit Your Reference List

An *Interview Turn-down* is an experience that can be worked on. For instance, you find yourself in the interview final-decision process several times and you are told, *we need to verify your references and we will get back to you*. Then, the next communication—whether a call from the recruiter or the company letter—arrives and it indicates that the position is no longer open. Maybe this is the case but, if it happens to you more than once, you may want to revisit your reference list.

As we stated before, references are very important. If you neglected to communicate with the references or neglected to review the correlation between what the company is asking and what the references are saying, this may be the area to examine.

If you recall, in Chapter 4 we stated that you need an arrangement with your references to call shortly after they have spoken with the employer. The information you learn may well be something that needs to be communicated to your other references, BEFORE they are contacted. In fact, it is a good idea to call references to determine progress—stay in touch with them!

Take a little time and visit with your references to see what you can learn. If by chance you discover that the company didn't even call your references (ouch), then go back to the mirror test and be honest with yourself as to what else could be happening.

Bottom line:
make your references an extension of yourself
—keep them on the dance floor!

Keep Selling Yourself

When we have done an interview review with clients, sometimes the issue was that they were too difficult in negotiation of the financial package—the client asked for more than the position was worth. They stopped selling themselves when told that they were on the candidate short list.

Remember, it is not over until it is over and you are, in fact, on the job—don't stop selling yourself before this time. Naturally, a point can be made that in the world of work, you never stop selling yourself.

Preparation is Key

Sometimes we found that the reason for a client being turned down was as simple as not being prepared in the delivery of the interview. A quick solution would be to have someone video tape an interview session and then you can review your responses to questions being asked and make corrections as observed.

The process of being turned down is hard for anyone to accept in most cases. The thing to do is pick up the pieces, learn from the experience and move on. You need to believe in yourself and what you are going to be able to do for a company that does hire you. It might turn out that you become the biggest competitor of the company who turned you down!

Remember this little story.
All great baseball hitters will tell you that they've
struck out more times than hit homeruns.
But that didn't stop them from
swinging at the pitches!

Possible Turndown Reasons

Of course, there are many other possibilities that exist. The following is a collection of potential turn-down reasons that surfaced while conducting our post-interviews and post-offer consulting.

Attitude	-displayed an overbearing attitude from the time of being greeted by the receptionist to and through the interview process -display of arrogance—you KNOW you are the perfect fit
Lack of Vitality	-looked tired: tired clothes, needed a haircut; -projected "tired" in the interview by slumping in the chair
Nervousness	-lack of confidence in delivery
Critical	-bad-mouthed previous employers; -condemned former supervisors or work environments
Lack of Presence	-eye contact lacking; -always looking down or away; -limp handshake
Unable to Defend Resume Statements	-if you put a statement on your resume YOU have to be able to define it, practice your answers, record them (best), use a video or ask a colleague if it sounds real and powerful
Relocation	-not wanting to relocate nor being open for it
Company Knowledge	-not able to display a depth of knowledge about the company
Enthusiasm	-just did not show enthusiasm for the opportunity
Personal Appearance	- perhaps you didn't dress appropriately for the interview; - gained a few pounds? think about getting a new suit or better yet, lose the weight; -do you have the current fashion apparel for interviewing; -are you projecting the image you want?

Presentation	-did not deliver a convincing presentation -did not use FAB effectively
Unprepared	-not ready to interview effectively -did not prepare and practice enough
Questions	-asked poorly thought-out questions

Maybe you just didn't perform the *dance of the interviewers* and therefore you need to prepare—prepare—prepare and practice—practice—practice.

Top 6 Reasons for Rejection

We received a *List of the Top Six Reasons Applicants Are Rejected.* This comes from a Fortune 50 Company and a hiring manager who deals with thousands of applicants:

1.   The perfect person - one who is so sure of himself that he never makes mistakes. He wouldn't consider a mistake a learning/growth opportunity.

2.   Body language - eye rolling, sighing, fidgeting. Sloppy in appearance.

3.   Candidate who wants to come to work everyday and "just do her job." She is not interested in learning/ doing anything beyond what is required, including overtime. She does not have any goals or future plans for advancement.

4.   Making excuses or blaming others for some incident in his current job that caused a conflict or problem. Someone unable to take or accept personal responsibility for his or her actions/ outcomes.

5.   Overselling qualifications - upon checking references it is learned that the candidate has inflated her perception of abilities.

6.   Candidate who is only interested in your job posting because he heard it was a fun/great place to work. He doesn't really care what the job is; he just wants to get in the company or the department.

The previous pages contain the main reasons for receiving an interview turn-down. Of course, there are more but these are areas that you can readily correct and make a difference in the outcome.

Lessons from Practice Interview Sessions

The following are some examples of clients in the interview practice sessions that we conducted. We tried to make *the interview* training as real as possible—a dress rehearsal (yes, including the interview clothes). These examples come as eye-openers—lessons about how *little things* as well as *big things* can make a difference in an interview.

The first case is about a person who came into the interview practice session chewing gum. He was not only chewing it but his mouth was opening up as he did his thing. After a couple of minutes it was obvious he was not aware of it and it wasn't going away. A small thing? Not really, because all we were able to do was focus on this chewing machine.

Gum-chewing distracts the interviewer(s)

So we stopped the taping, suggested he throw it away and explained what it was doing to us. He started laughing as he told us he really doesn't chew gum but, he had talked to another client who was previously taped and said it made him so nervous that (being a smoker) he got some Nicotine Gum to use during the interview so he could relax.

The next story is a lesson in remembering that everyone is watching you when you go to the interview. The setting was the reception area; we had the clients come to the interview just like they would have to do at a company, which means waiting in the reception area. Well this client, instead of asking to be excused for a quick trip to the ladies' room, proceeded to do her make-up refreshing in the reception area.

When we discussed it in the feedback session, she said:

> *I know; I have never done that in public before.*
> *I am always late for appointments and I didn't*
> *want to be late for this session.*

Personal grooming should
be done in private.

Another person waved their hands so much we ducked a few times thinking a hit was coming. Know your body language (video tape) and practice a replacement for something that appears to take away from your presentation. Always remember that for a bad habit to go away (stop) you have to replace it with a good habit.

Consider that your body language
may be distracting.

Sometimes applicants aren't aware of the tension created by interviewing, especially if they haven't done a lot of it. This client (if you can visualize this) was nervous and was shaking his leg under the table. He was not aware of the action his body was taking to release the pressure. Unfortunately, it also traveled up through the rest of his body and sitting in front of us was the bouncing client.

This is why we say make sure you are prepared and get the practice, practice and practice. After reviewing the tape, he did deal with it by practicing and through a different mindset that gave him confidence—then he actually looked forward to interviews.

A very intense accountant was in the interview role-play session and he constantly blinked his eyes to such a degree it caused us to focus on his blinking (looked like fish eyes) and not what he was saying.

In our debriefing, we asked if he wore contacts and he said yes, but only to interviews because he had very thick glasses. He said he had his glasses with him and we asked him to go change. We again filmed some more footage and the problem went away and his glasses looked fine on him. He immediately started to get follow-up second interviews.

Another situation to be aware of is one of over-confidence. You don't want to appear arrogant in the interview and display an attitude that tells the interviewer that you don't feel like you have to work to demonstrate your candidacy. Perhaps even worse, is the over-confident person who is not open to advice. Remember, the chance at a follow-up interview will be lost if you don't make the right dance steps nor pay attention to the music!

Over-confidence can appear as arrogance!

You have to believe that there is a job for everyone, a job you will want to accept. You have to keep looking to discover it, stay the course, and keep working with your network and resources. And remember: watch for those little habits!

COACHES CORNER II

How to Find Search Firms and Recruiters

AT THE TOP OF the list for locating search firms and employment agencies is your personal network. It is possible that you will be able to secure names of firms or recruiters, along with their reputation, from among your network contacts, such as friends and colleagues.

Another possibility is the HR department that covered your severance—these people work with recruiters all the time. You can ask them for some names of recruiters and if they would refer you for credibility purposes. This way the company is saying you are okay. It's worth a try even if you learn that the HR manager is not willing to do it.

The logic behind this initial form of sourcing for recruiters is that, in most cases, if you are unemployed, the recruiters are not going to call you at home until you have a relationship with them.

At work, you are in a better position to be contacted for an opportunity. If the recruiters are doing sourcing (headhunting—sorry, recruiters), they are calling places of employed individuals.

They may cold-call a person as a resource who can refer other people or they may try to recruit the person they are sourcing. Often in today's electronic times the recruiter will send mailings (hard copy) telling of open positions or use the Internet to advertise potential openings.

Use Your Network

The ideal situation occurs when you meet with your network contacts: you can close the meeting by asking them if they know of any recruiters to whom they can refer you. If they do have a referral of a recruiter, always ask if you can use their name (better to be referred by someone). So, as part of your professional contacts always remember to ask them if they have any contacts with search firms/ agencies that they would recommend.

Searching for Recruiters

If you are not blessed with the above contacts and referrals then you will need to go exploring on your own. One reference is called *The Directory of Executive Recruiters*, often referred to as the "Red Book;" you may find you have to spend a little time getting used to the indexing system in this book. This reference will enable you to select firms that may be of interest.

It will also help if you are looking to relocate or plan to do multi-tasking and search a specific geographical area other than your current locale. If you are a recent transfer to the company always remember to call back to your former city, and maybe company, for referrals. I am sure they will still remember you.

Find information on the internet or even the yellow pages under employment and/ or consultants; you can make some selections that seem to fit assignments in your industry or background. In reading the classified advertisements, pay attention to the ads that are placed by agencies—even if the ads are not for your skills. Names of recruiters may be in the ad. You can call to see if their area of recruiting may include positions for you or if they can refer you to another recruiter. You can also check with the local Chamber of Commerce.

To save you time later, take a few minutes and learn how to use these references appropriately. If it seems foreign to you, try to network with a recruiter who is willing to give you a short course in using a search firm or an employment agency.

There are several ways to locate
the right recruiters.

As you get into using search firms, it is not important to be concerned about where they are located, as most search recruiters will travel to companies for business. They are retained to locate the ideal candidate, in most cases regardless of where the candidate lives. With employment agencies the opposite is true; they normally are located in the city that they serve. They may be part of a national network, but the local recruiter is the best bet if you are trying to stay local.

The search firm, as a rule of measure, will not engage a search for less than $100,000. On the other hand the local employment agency will work around the ranges of $25-$40,000 and $40-$80,000. Then there are the temp-to-perm firms, which recruit people to start a position as a temporary worker. Then after a period of time (usually 90 days) may offer up a permanent position. Note: these assignments normally do not include benefits.

As a rule:
Search Firms focus on the + $100 000 salary
Employment Agencies: $25-40 000 & $40-80 000 level
Temp-to-Perm firms for starting positions

By chance you begin thinking that you may work part-time while you are looking for full-time—think this through carefully! You may be doing yourself a disservice as the part-time job can take away from the time you need to manage and work your new job search activities. On the other hand, it could be a way for you to start with a company and prove yourself for a full-time position.

It is worth mentioning that in some companies it is a practice to recruit a temporary executive to head up a COO, CFO or CEO position, providing a contract for a year or more. Most of these firms can be found on the Internet and the largest number are located in Stamford, CT and Chicago, IL.

Remember to keep this in mind while preparing your contact list of recruiters: By virtue of what this third party does serves as a unique perspective in the hiring activities of most companies. It should pay dividends if you spend time cultivating a working relationship with a few selected firms/recruiters.

COACHES CORNER III

Working with Search Firms and Employment Agencies

FIRST AND FOREMOST—REMEMBER that search firms and employment agencies work for the employer. Career advice and employment decisions received from these firms must be kept in perspective; factor in your own knowledge and experience when considering their information. You may find exceptions, for instance, when you work with a professional recruiter who has previously placed you into a company, or someone you know from your business dealings—these contacts can be a real asset to your networking process.

If a search firm has been retained by a company and is acting as the agent, it is in their own best interests to work as diligently as possible with you—they do not want to have to start the search again if you happen to turn down the opportunity.

While with a previous company, you may have received calls from recruiters for business, or in some cases, looking for specific job applicants. If you have been friendly to them or even gave them some help they will not forget that. Call and remind them of favors in the past. However, if you were rude, they will also remember that for a long, long time!

Retainer Firms

There are basically two broad types of recruiting firms: retainer firms and contingency firms. The retainer firms are paid by the company on a retainer arrangement to recruit qualified people for specific positions. Most of these firms begin their engagement at the $100k+ level. The retainer fee plus expenses will average around 40% of the hired person's total earnings (usually including any additional forms of compensation) for the first year.

Contingency Firms

The contingency firms work on a commission basis and are paid when the individual they present is *hired and starts*. In most cases the hiring company will not make these assignments exclusive. As you begin working with contingency firms you may find several of them are working with the same company and their open positions. The contingency firm will ask which companies you have been in contact with and how far along you are in the interview process. They simply don't want to duplicate the effort.

Caution needs to be taken here—the recruiter can work against you by taking the company and open position information and utilizing it to send other candidates. That's why building trust in a recruiter or having a referral from someone you know is better than a cold call. If *cold calls* are all you have, go for it; it is much better than sitting and waiting for calls to come after flooding the market with all your resumes. This leads to another point: if you have a good network, the recruiters may become a secondary source for you.

Some other pertinent information about contingency firms: the cost to the hiring company will be approximately 20–30 percent or 1% per thousand dollars of income or your just-starting salary. There is usually a 60-90 day guarantee and this can extend to six months—the guarantee means the employment agency needs to provide a replacement if the job doesn't work out. If you decide to leave the company on your own (not because of downsizing or for an EEOC reason through no fault by you), the agency could charge you for the fee expenses. This can vary by state just as employment "at will" does. It is essential to take few minutes of your time to research this information.

We have always recommended that if the employment agency asks you to sign something in order to work with you, *make sure you know what you are signing.* In most cases we have advised not to sign anything related to your job search representation by agencies to companies—a handshake will work, or negotiate the arrangement. Always ask if this is a fee-paid position, meaning the company pays the fee. A good book to reference in how to work with search firms is *Rites of Passage* (2000) authored by John Lucht, a professional retained recruiter.

Always ensure you know what you are signing!

Generally speaking most companies prefer not to pay a fee for searching for qualified applicants in the job market. Their first choices are: employee referral, industry referral from a friend, and becoming more prevalent, the use of the Internet.

It is also noteworthy that there are companies who benefit greatly by using a firm as it can reduce the time of recruiting. Without a strong recruiting department a company could make hiring mistakes and increase the time it takes to fill the position, or hire the wrong person altogether—using recruiting firms makes good business sense. If there happens to be an up-turn economic situation where there are more jobs than qualified people, recruiters become very valuable for finding applicants. Of course the opposite is true if there is a downturn economically as companies want to spend less.

Again, on the average, most contingency firms work at middle management or specific technical positions. As we have stated before, there has been a trend in some companies' hiring practices to operate a temp-to-perm arrangement with the candidate. Simply, you get hired as a temporary employee and after a period of time, usually based on performance, you are asked to become a permanent employee.

We have advised our clients to utilize their network of friends and company contact referrals as a beginning source for identifying recruiters or search firms. In the network meeting as you have finished the discussion of your background and what you are looking for, you can ask if they could recommend a recruiter or recruiting firm they may have utilized. This is an excellent resource since the firm is known and you can ask to use the referral's name when contacting the firm.

Recruiters and Your Job Campaign

The middle-of-the-road approach to using recruiters as part of your campaign is the best way to budget your time. The specific number of recruiters to use usually depends upon many personal variables. To recommend how many firms to use and what type is left up to you. What number of recruiters feels comfortable will become very apparent as you develop your job search plan.

As in any job search plan, focus your efforts to get a good return. It's not advisable to blindly send resumes and cover letters to randomly selected firms (mass mailings). Again, the best approach is using past knowledge, next, a referral, then through research using reference materials dealing with the available recruiting firms.

We also discussed these approaches in *identifying search firms* in Coaches Corner II. Remember the usage and success rate of the Internet is growing bigger everyday.

Not to consider the possibility of using the employment agency or search firm needs to be evaluated; to entirely overlook the recruiter community as a potentially valuable resource in securing a meaningful position could be a shortcoming in your job search campaign. The current edition of *The Directory of Executive Recruiters* has reference sections advising how to work with firms.

Approaching a Recruiter

Once you have collected and organized your recruiter contact list (again, how many you need will be determined by your job search plan) you can begin with a direct approach—if you have a phone number, call the company or, if the search firm is located in your city, there is nothing wrong with walking through the front door and asking to speak to someone—it is very hard to ignore someone in your lobby!

Another recommendation is sending your cover letter and resume addressed to a specific recruiter by name. Use e-mail (without attachments), posted mail, and sometimes FAX.

Realistically, you need to take into consideration that many of the larger or better-known firms receive such a volume of applicant contacts that you may have to try different tactics as time goes by. This is no different from using the Internet to apply for positions as your application for a posted position goes into a black hole. Law of averages dictates that there is a resume gridlock on the Internet due to a few reasons: there are more applicants than jobs; it is easier to apply on the Internet; and, there is a feeling of accomplishment when posting a resume—so more people are apt to use this venue.

The important issue is not the number of resumes you have sent out or posted, it's the number of companies you've talked to, and/or with which you've had an interview of some sort. Companies are beginning to use the Internet more than traditional classified advertisement.

There is more information to consider about the market. The economy will always have its up-and-down activity as to the number of jobs compared to applicants available. There will always be some form of downsizing utilized by companies. The increases in outsourcing/downsizing are a direct outcome of mergers or acquisitions—the result is duplication and consolidation of positions and therefore, excess employees. If the baby boomers decide to bail out of the work force in these next several decades, employers will be faced with the difficulty of a shortage of qualified people to employ or to replace the exiting boomers.

The outsourcing of jobs overseas will continue to some degree—it's cost effective and a large consumer of goods. Some industries will pull back after trying this tactic because it may not be productive or financially sound for them. The workweek will continue to increase for salaried employees (about an average of 50 hours now) to get their job done.

It is believed by some executives that this trend increases productivity and can reduce the need for additional hiring (people are doing more than one job). However, it has been proven time and time again that this house of cards will come down. Today many working professionals are taking a more serious look at quality of life issues and family involvement. There are many social issues that are being linked back to working environments; these will impact the world of work, and many changes can follow.

Other Options

Now don't get discouraged, there is a job for everyone, we just have to find it. You will get called to interview if your background is a match for the needs of an ongoing recruiting assignment. If you have read this book this far, you will also know that we recommend multi-sourcing the job market.

One area of job search that is increasing is direct contact and referral to a company with which you have an interest. This also includes researching or reading about a company in the media—realizing that you could benefit them and apply direct even if there are no openings posted.

As the economy improves it will become less of a risk to relocate to where the jobs are. Again, as applicant shortages develop, more companies will begin to pick-up the relocation costs. As couples continue to have dual incomes and grow in their professional occupations, there will be a direct impact on relocation in terms of affordability and who decides who quits their job. Makes for interesting family career discussions.

It is worth noting that due to the cost and labor expense, employment agencies and search firms are sending fewer status letters. More often today it will be in the form of a postcard or e-mail. This holds true in most cases when applying to government openings. Apparently less than 1/3 of their contacts received any status information. Often clients had to pursue the information.

When you have been contacted and have completed the first screening interview, the identity of the client company will most likely not be divulged. Nevertheless, you usually get enough information from being interviewed, coupled with your networking, to determine the name of the company. In the case of professional search firms, if they feel you are qualified, the company info comes sooner.

You will find through experience that the amount of time a recruiter will give you is usually related to how marketable you are. If they are working on a number of assignments similar to your background, they may send you out on interviews immediately. Remember first impressions are critical in your first contact and/ or interview with recruiters.

If by chance you are really inexperienced in working with recruiters, employment agencies of all types and/ or search firms, it can be valuable to completely read our book, review a book dedicated to working with recruiters, engage a career consultant or contact a friend who has knowledge of the process. Always keep in mind that employment agencies work on a numbers game and make their money by placing as many individuals as possible.

Try to avoid having your resume hung out in the market like clothes on a line as this may be viewed by companies that you are desperate or indiscriminate in your job search. How resumes are handled should be part of your discussion with the agency.

Lastly, don't allow yourself to be pushed into taking a job either by the company or employment agency—you are the decision maker and you can say no if it's not in your best interest. Good luck in your quest.

Developing Your Market Plan

COMPANIES WHO WANT TO launch and successfully market a product need a well-thought-out marketing plan. The marketing plan starts with research about the branding or what the product has to offer in terms of Features—Advantages—Benefits (FAB) in order to get the customer to the buying stage and ultimately, a decision. The marketing plan will provide direction to the company and effectively manage their time. So, what is your plan?

Marketing Yourself

As we have coached clients who were not as familiar or comfortable working with marketing terms, we helped them by giving examples of branding or marketing plans that are similar to their business planning or objectives/ goals. When you start looking for a job, it's like launching a product, except in this case the *product is you*. You develop your FAB:

- Features—key behaviors
- Advantages—skills/ job knowledge
- Benefits—how your behaviors meet or solve the position's needs and problems

In order to do this successfully do some research and learn how to market yourself. Invest time to learn as much as you can about potential buyers (employers) and what will appeal to them. What are the advantages and disadvantages? As we have discussed earlier, it is a good idea to have a written list of accomplishments, employment history, career decisions, skills and behaviors you are selling.

Investigate the Market

Become an investigative reporter and develop the who, what, where, and why. We have advised clients with problems developing a marketing plan to try a new tactic—use the following questions as a start. This strategy often helped draw a picture and the client could visualize some of the steps to help develop their re-employment plan.

- is my interest regional or local? Do the companies I am interested in have a presence locally? Do I have to consider looking more regional? Are there specific locations of the industry I want to approach?

  If relocating is not an option, then this will affect your plan—what will be your fall-back plan?

- who is the hiring authority or how do I find him? Is he local or located at another location?

- how do I make contact with the company without getting lost in a sea of resumes?

- what looks most promising for me to begin with or use in resources—start with the area in which I have the most knowledge? What is my network like?

- what are the salary ranges, how does this compare to mine?

- what will my workweek look like as to my timeline. When do I need a job? *Determine the realistic date and then work back to the present.* What do I have to do to meet that date? Is this realistic? *It's better to know now than later when the options are fewer and the debts are bigger.*

- set-up some measurable goals and review them weekly. *It is easy to feel a sense of accomplishment by applying to ten jobs on the Internet and not work with your other resources. Clients who managed their time accordingly, used all their contacts/ resources, and didn't limit themselves to the Internet, usually had the best returns for the effort that was invested.*

- answer this question—what will prevent me from being hired? salary? location? experience level? performance in the interview?

With the information and framework above, now consider the development of your marketing plan to launch yourself.

COACHES CORNER V

Sample Interview Questions

FOCUS YOUR INTERVIEW PREPARATION on developing the capability to answer questions of the interviewers. In post interviews, often applicants expressed disappointment if interviewers weren't as prepared as they were, or if the interview session seemed poorly administered. They were prepared and anxious to experience a good interview in order to deliver their candidacy for the opportunity. The applicants sometimes found it difficult to follow the line of questioning and had to labor to get some of their key background information across to the interviewer.

A common complaint was: *I had to interject several times an example of my prior work experience to the interviewer.* This is a classic case of when to use a short story presentation of your background overview in order to give the interviewer a snapshot of you. So, regardless of how well the company conducts their interviews, it is your job to get the message from your side to their side of the table!

Some caution here is important—don't develop a completely passive approach to the interview session. *Always ensure you are prepared.* You could say something to the interviewer, like: "Would you like me to give you a brief overview of my work experiences and background?" Or, another strategy: just let the interviewer talk—nod, smile, or ask questions when appropriate and at the end, suggest providing a brief overview.

There will be challenging interviews as some companies have learned how valuable a professional interviewer is for hiring the right person. As we described in Chapter One, interviewing is a science and an art, with experience thrown in to compensate for "Murphy's Law." Most applicants are able to acquire enough skill and ability to perform well enough in the interview process to secure a position. There are some clients who have clearly seen the advantage a future executive can have in developing and fine-tuning the various interview circumstances they face.

In personal and professional settings the interview is a valuable tool to learn. At home in relationships, whether social or managing, and when information or investigative data gathering, the interview process can be a real asset. After all, it is just a matter of knowing yourself and being able to tell someone about the real YOU!

Forms of Interviewing

Let's discuss a form of interviewing used by some companies and referred to as targeted selection or behavior-based questioning. The work world has discovered that past behavior is a good predictor of future behavior. It requires the interviewer to truly know the critical skills of the open position, the culture (behavioral fit), as well as understand how the position interfaces with the rest of the organization.

This form of interviewing usually requires the applicant be interviewed by a number of employees who represent a vertical slice of the company. The applicant will be interviewed by: a person who is employed higher in the organization than the open position, some peers or staff, and at least one person at the same level. At the same time, to expedite the interview schedule, the HR department will sometimes arrange a group interview (2 to 3 individuals) or sequential interviews.

Today the interviews are becoming lengthier, some lasting longer than an hour. One way to be better prepared is to call in advance, ask how many people and with whom (along with titles) you will be interviewing. Titles are important because they provide information that will enable you to anticipate and formulate questions based on that person's interest and how your position will impact their area.

Some of these interview programs will be scored. The answer you give should be in the format we advised you to use while completing your accomplishments: **SARB** or Situation, Actions, Results and Behaviors/ attitudes:

- What was the <u>Situation</u> or problem?
- What <u>Actions</u> were taken: beginning with what decisions you made, what you did to address or solve the problem or situation?
- What was the outcome or <u>Results</u> obtained (quantify)?
- What personal <u>Behaviors</u> went into the process?

Most technical licenses/ degrees/ certifications are usually handled early in the interview process and then references checked after or during the hiring process. The macro areas that will be explored with specific questions are:

- general subjects, small talk;
- how problems were approached and resolved;
- communication skills;
- motivation;
- self-awareness;
- interpersonal skills/ team development;
- management/ change environments/ administration;
- knowledge of your industry today and future considerations.

You cannot anticipate every question but you will be ready for most interview situations if you:

- prepare your responses;
- practice difficult questions;
- feel comfortable with your accomplishments;
- know your behaviors—the REAL you!

Sample Questions and Answers

Now let's look at some sample interview questions. As you consider each of these, think about the role your SARBs play into each.

What are you looking for in a job?

Briefly review your desire to concentrate on doing the position well and having the opportunity to use your skills. Then state that you're confident that the future will be promising. If it is early in the interview process don't assume you know enough about the position to state unrealistic goals.

What is it about this job that is attractive to you?

State that, based upon what you have learned about this opportunity, it meets your ideal work parameters and then relate it to some examples of where and how you can benefit the position. This is also a good time to state how you are able to use job knowledge and to meet or exceed business objectives.

In what specific areas of knowledge required by this job do you feel especially experienced?

Remember you have to have sufficient information about the wants and needs of the position. This is the time to express your strongest job skills or job knowledge. Answer with 2 to 3 of your major skills—matched to their needs—and then give an accomplishment to support what you stated.

What accomplishments are you able to bring to this position from your previous company? Overall in your career what has been your greatest achievement so far?

The interviewer is trying to measure your behaviors for this position and the team. You should have at least 2 to 3 areas from your research that you can deliver, plus, always base your answer on what you have learned of the priorities/ values for this position. This is a time to use SARB. Frame your response to meet these goals, get the behavior message across and then stop talking.

Or, a different way of asking the same question:

What key skills do you possess that will help you do this job?

Review your principle job knowledge and behaviors: your management style, decision-making, leadership and team play (whatever applies to the job). Give examples, if you can, from your previous experience that mirrors their needs.

Share with us a time and situation where your work was criticized. How did you recover?

Carefully practice a response ahead of time so that you deliver in a positive tone. Have one example and how you learned from the feedback. Also include what you learned from this event. If you actually don't have an example, discuss how or what you would do if it had happened.

Tell us about a time when the team you were part of did not agree with you and the direction you wanted to go.

One possible response is: *The team was encouraged to present their reasoning and other pertinent information. Next, I shared the thoughts and reasoning behind my decision. We were then able to see how close our thinking was. Because some of the contributions made were worthy of consideration, I explained how we could incorporate these into the decision. The fact that they felt comfortable sharing their feelings was impressive and so I commended them for it.*

Is there a time when you disagreed with your supervisor? What did you do and what was the outcome?

In this case give a situation, indicate you welcomed the input from the supervisor and sometimes changed his mind. If he said his way was still the way to go, you supported him fully.

What kind of employees do you find it difficult to work with and why?

You want to take your time answering this question. Keep your answer realistic. Refer to your management style and what you do to ensure you can work with all employees. How do you approach conflict resolution?

Describe how you would handle a subordinate's poor performance or at least those areas where you think better work can be done.

Give one example. Describe the private meeting with the employee with specific examples of specific areas. Explain how you got a commitment from the employee and provided a measurable improvement objective with a time line. And, tell how it turned out.

If we were to speak with your peer group what would they say about what it was like to work with you?

Go to your strengths and behaviors that have been discussed with your peers. Be honest as references can be checked.

How would your former boss describe your management decision-making? Your results?

Draw upon a couple of examples from your accomplishments that reflect decision-making and state the results. Remember your performance reviews. Remember that SARBs are your answers in many, if not all, interview situations.

What in your opinion makes you effective in one-to-one relationships and working with a team? Please give examples.

Refer to a past situation where you can state your management style and point out the difference in managing the two types of groups. Important components to include: setting measurable goals with timeline, synergy, achieving company's goals, and cooperation. A behavior discussion is important to opinion-type questions.

How would you describe your personality?

This is one of those behavior questions (like others: management style, decision-making) that deals with your opinion/ behavior and helps identify your fit into the company. From your research, you will know the company's mission statement. Tie your behaviors to their mission statement.

Describe for us how you would go about planning for a major change that would not put you in a favorable light. What would your communications style be?

A strong response to this question should include discussing the following: make sure of the facts and secure your manager's support. Communicate with each area impacted and get them to understand their role, discuss change issues, don't blame the company or find fault. Try to get agreement to look toward the future.

In your previous position what did you like the most? Least?

As you did your accomplishment review, you most likely also

found some preferences, likes, or dislikes. Address the positives and then chose a 'least liked' that can put you in a favorable light. Again, you should carefully practice your answer to give the right impression.

Example: *In my last job I disliked the lack of completeness in management decisions. At times an order was given only to be later altered. However, while I dislike this, I am good at coping and dealing with ambiguity. I work hard at thinking and reasoning.*

In the next five years what priorities do feel our industry will be facing?

Relate your research and personal experiences. Mention a couple of challenges that can lead to success/ market share. You may have information in your Briefing Book that you could share and demonstrate your thoroughness.

What was the last business book you have read? What have you done or are doing to keep developing your skills?

Relate some training you have had, seminars, a business book read or you are reading—that in some way relates to the industry. Keep it non-controversial.

What kind of decisions do you find difficult to make and why?

A couple good possibilities are: having to let someone go for job performance; not having all the information needed to make what you feel is a strong decision. Immediately follow up with an explanation of what you would do in that case.

Where do you prefer to spend your time: planning operations or implementing them?

Make sure your answer relates to the position for which you

are interviewing. Point out that both skills are needed in most cases. Think balance!

What has been your track record in hiring, training, promoting, and firing employees?

Hiring is one of the critical functions of a manager and this fact should be used in the answer. Also, since people hire people in their own image, it gives you a great opportunity to get a personal message out! Of course, make sure you refer to your performance in these areas and summarize, e.g./ *In the last five years I have hired approximately __ and some of these employees went into management. I have only had to fire __ employees.* You will also need to anticipate a *why* question about the firing of employees.

If you could start your career again, what changes would you make?

Again relate to a real situation. Or, in most cases explain that you have made good progress and expect to continue with the same. That's why you are excited about this position.

Describe for us a situation where you had to work under a tight deadline. Have you ever failed to bring a project in on time and on budget?

Refer to a real accomplishment (SARB) from your background. If you also brought in a project ahead of time and under budget, be sure to get this in also.

What level of budget and financial experiences do you have? Have you been responsible for P/ L? What has been the largest budget that you have managed?

Now remember as you get closer to the specific area of the

company you are going to be in charge of (or will have impact on), some of the questions will be specific to that responsibility: Sales – Sales Management – Marketing – CFO – COO – CEO – Public Relations – Legal – R & D – Information Technology – Manufacturing – General Manager – HR – Administration.

What is the difference between leadership and management?

Describe 2-3 differences and be prepared to give an accomplishment (or SARB) as a follow-up. For example:

- leadership is the ability to influence the actions and opinions of others in a desired direction and to exhibit judgment in leading others to worthwhile objectives;
- management is overseeing the operation: she is the supervisor who guides and controls;
- the manager deals with the trees one by one and the leader deals with the whole forest;
- a good manager will also have some leadership characteristics.

Are you close to a decision or expecting an offer from another company?

Indicate you are actively interviewing as they would expect, but you don't need to tell them you have another offer coming at this time; this could dampen or hurt your chances with them. Once you have the offer or you do have more than one offer, plan out how you are going to close the deal. The sticky part comes when you know you are just at the front door with the one company and about to receive an offer from another.

Sometimes, if you are a stellar applicant they may push for a quicker completion of the interview process. You will know and sense when you have to begin discussing both offers. Remember it is in your best interest to get what you want.

How soon do you feel you can
make a contribution?

A good response will be a form of the following: *With my background and experiences I can begin making some form of contribution almost immediately.* Be prepared for follow-up questions asking you to provide more specific information.

As I look at your background and accomplishments,
it appears to me you would be
over-qualified or too experienced for this job.

What they may be thinking is that you are desperate. Reflect back to a goal they want accomplished and explain that you bring the kind of experience necessary to reach that goal. Point out benefits like: the learning and results curve could be shorter and additional skills are available that the manager can use.

How much do you feel you are worth? Or, how much do
you expect to earn if we offer this position to you?

You expect to be paid fairly in relation to the amount of responsibility. If pushed for an answer, go to your research information on salary averages for the position and say you are looking for a position that pays in the range of x-x. Then ask for the range of this position, or if they feel that you fall into the range of this position.

We have included information on negotiation and steps you can take; refer to Coaches Corner XII and Chapter 10 in the text.

Remember confidence is important in your
delivery. Believe yourself!

Get plenty of rest before the
interview. Vitality or energy level can make
a difference in your answers and how you
are perceived.

Try to sit in a straight-backed chair,
avoid soft furniture and greet everyone,
including those in the reception areas.

Prepare, video tape yourself and
practice—practice—practice.

COACHES CORNER VI

References

THROUGHOUT THIS BOOK WE have mentioned the importance of references, and in Chapter Four the topic was explored in detail. In this Coaches Corner section, we provide a sample checklist and a few examples of skills and abilities that you can use.

Examples of Job Skills:

Personnel
-scheduling
-teaching/ training
-course development
-contract negotiation

Technical
-MS Office products

Marketing
-ad strategies
-copy writing
-integrated marketing

Telecommunications
-call center management

Financial
-accounting software
-wage administration
-budgeting
-P/L management

Government Regulations

Don't forget your accomplishments! Utilize references to reinforce and support accomplishments.

Examples of Behaviors:

Effective listener	Self-motivation
Integrity	Strong work ethic
Caring	Enthusiasm
Flexible	Reliable
Problem solver	Team work
Leadership	Initiative
Adaptable	People skills

Remember to choose behaviors that can be reinforced and supported by personal references. For instance, one person may feel that you are decisive while another may point to communication skills as your real strength—the important thing is that references are able to support the examples you choose.

When you develop a reference list, you are interested in those people who can reinforce, and those who are able to support examples of your job skills. Another point to consider is the inclusion of personal references: someone who knows your behaviors. You may be asked for a personal reference—be prepared by listing one or two in your Briefing Book.

**Sample format for preparing your reference list
on following page:**

Reference Names			
Define the relationship (e.g. peer, supervisor, team member, professional relationship)			
How long have you known this person?			
What is the nature of your working relationship?			
How does this person impact or relate to your career?			
Can this person support the reason you left the organization?			
Is this person able to summarize or discuss your work/ performance?			

COACHES CORNER VII

Developing Cover Letters

JOB SEARCH CORRESPONDENCE is of key importance for your job search campaign. A basic rule for sending a resume is: always use a cover letter. You can imagine all the resumes or letters of inquiry a company may receive. Using a cover letter is like having a map available on a road trip. It leads the reader to where you want her. Actually many recruiters won't consider an applicant if a cover letter isn't included. Often these recruiters will pre-scan the resume mail received in order to reduce the number to read—noting whether or not there is a cover letter is a tool to accomplish this objective.

Basics of a Good Cover Letter

Your cover letter should be in a well-written format. Use the letter to create focus, interest and attention by highlighting your unique skills and work accomplishments. This letter creates the first impression for consideration as an applicant. It is a great opportunity to draw attention to your qualifications. Remember the goal of a cover letter is to secure an interview and with continued interview success, a new position.

What is considered to be a good cover letter? To make your cover letter stand out make sure you know the pertinent facts about the type of work you do. While writing, try to put yourself in the position of the employer: what is he really looking for? How does this opportunity compare with what you are looking for in a new position? Try to read between the lines of the ad or Internet posting and decide what pertinent information could make your background more interesting to the employer. Here are some questions to ask yourself:

- Which behaviors make me particularly well suited for this position?
- What specific words will create interest about my experiences/ accomplishments?
- What accomplishment examples should I include to demonstrate specific skills and abilities?
- How can I show sensitivity to/ or understanding of the company's needs?

Don't forget: If someone referred you, include the name.

Include a Post Script (P.S.) in closing. This has worked as a bell ringer for clients and last thing remembered about your potential benefit to the organization. Postscripts usually are written in the form of an accomplishment statement.

The following demonstrate pertinent information to include in your cover letter. Remember, while the letter may not get the reader's total focus, it seems that the P.S. is read 100% of the time!

Key Topics to Include

A cover letter should include these key topics:

- your interest in the company/ position;
- examples of why the company should be interested in you;
- suggestion of the next steps you can take; and
- remember the P.S.

Develop each letter separately—each must be individualized—with managers' names or names from your network contacts. All cover letters are addressed to an individual in the company's management team or the HR manager. Call the company to obtain this name. Brevity of the letter is key.

Include Pertinent Information

The following are examples of statements you can use or adapt for a cover letter. Note that each is brief yet very powerful in terms of seizing the attention of the reader.

While doing your research it may become clear where you can benefit the company immediately:

- A key strength that I will bring to your company is . . .
- My resume contains some key accomplishments related to the company. One is experience . . . (e.g. reducing costs).

Another tactic, and a very good one, is to open with a question that gets the attention of the reader. For example:

- Is part of your strategic plan to develop International Sales?
- Are today's labor costs eating into your profits?

You have developed your network contacts and are fortunate to be able to use a name of contact—this makes for a powerful tool.

- _____ of World-wide Sales, Inc. recommended that I contact you about a senior Sales Manager position in your new European Division.
- I met _____ at a recent convention (subject was: _____). He suggested that I would be a natural for your company. _____ said he was going to call you.

If you have access to a job description or Internet posting, you are in a position to compare your background to the advertised needs.

> The description of the job in your ad suggests that you are looking for a person with proven _____ ("experience" can be used, but it is such a common word; think of another descriptor like "proven corporate impact" and be as specific as possible).

As you do your research, you may find the company is in the news. Try to make a connection between your successes and the news report.

> I recently read about your merger with _____; I have key experience in this process.

In the beginning, it may seem to take a lot of time to do these letters, but it will pay dividends. Actually once you develop several types you will be able to speed the process along. When applying on the Internet, remember to include a short cover letter in your e-mails.

One letter style does not fit all the needs for communicating, following up, or presenting information to the potential employer. Answering ads, thank-you notes to personal meetings, contact letters and targeted company letters are types of correspondence for which to plan.

On the next few pages we've provided some examples of correspondence, but don't stop there—you can find a wealth of samples on the Internet to reference. Think about it! If you are not confident about this type of written communication you may want to purchase a cover letter book to help you build a foundation—then design the letter to reflect current styles.

Good luck with all of your correspondence—including your acceptance letter.

1. Letter with resume in response to advertisement

Rule #1: always do the research so that you can address the letter to an individual;

Rule #2: don't rush to get a response into the mail. You don't want your letter to arrive with the bulk of mail—waiting almost assures your letter will get a closer look.

---

123 Some Place
Indianapolis, IN 47923
(555) 325.8574

October 11, 2008

Barbara Hellow
HerbCon
123 Some Avenue
Minneapolis, MN 12345

Dear Ms Hellow,

The advertisement for junior marketing position in *Fine Products Journal* appears to require a success record, similar to what I have accomplished.

In my research, it was clear that HerbCon's culture consists of maintaining high intellectual oriented staff and is highly oriented towards developing effective teams. My accomplishments have demonstrated skills in the areas of innovative and conceptual thinking. In addition my accomplishments include the ability to develop teams which have a high attachment to their work and the company.

- Developed the idea to change a product's color scheme resulting in a 10% increase in sales;
- Identified a key recurring theme in employee turnover resulting in a turnover reduction by 5% annually;
- Restructured a communication process for a team resulting in a 20% increase of new ideas involving work flow.

I will call you in a few days to follow up on this letter.

Sincerely,

2. Marketing letter without resume

Marketing letter or "cold contact" is sent to create curiosity. Do not provide a lot of detail, but enough to give a solid picture of yourself.

This letter type is used for a target company you've developed from research and it is sent without a resume.

Dear

After completing extensive research on your company, I recognized that my background could be a good fit for your Sales and Marketing department.

While at Allergan Pharmaceutical, as an Area Sales Manager, my performance permitted us to achieve new market growth of 18%, or $12.5 million. In addition a newly created 360 degree feedback program resulted in achieving 100% employee retention, in its first year, and also resulted in the clear attachment of sales representatives to their positions, and to the company.

It is satisfying to be recognized as a sales executive with an eye on the future, and a history of turning around poor performing operations, as well as having job skills in P&L management, cost control, new product launches, negotiations and contract closure, and business planning.

From a personal competency/ behavior point of view, my success habits include: being innovative, recognizing customer needs, effective communication, developing workable initiatives, empowerment of people and the abilities to be self-reflective and self-correcting.

I will call you within the next four days and hopefully the opportunity will be there to allow me to discover how my experiences may fit your company.

Sincerely,

PS: Have a proven track record of developing outstanding sales teams and developing strategic initiatives.

3. A thank-you letter

Dear

Thank you again, the time we spent together was greatly appreciated as well as informative.

Our discussion about HamConn, and your needs for the position of customer relations coordinator sharpened my interest in working with you.

Your search for an individual who has been successful in building and maintaining teams, is a good match for my success in the area of teaming:

- Developed the trust of my team resulting in a 40% increase in accuracy.
- Increased a team's attachment to their work and to the company, reducing turnover by 15% by influencing and creating an effective collaboration atmosphere.

Those types of successes demonstrate my effectiveness with teams and for the company.

I am very interested in bringing those skills to HamConn. As you suggested, I will call in a few days to follow-up and I look forward to our next opportunity to visit.

Sincerely,

PS: Your keen interest in building cross functional relationships with teams is also an area in which success has been achieved.

The focus of any letter is to tie your candidacy to the needs of the company. A thank-you letter as follow-up to the interview is a great opportunity to clarify any part(s) of the interview which you feel might have been miscommunicated or misunderstood — giving personal examples to offset any perceived negatives.

4. Thank-you letter or thank-you card?

A written thank-you of some kind is always welcomed by an interviewer/ company. While many consider it a common courtesy, thank-yous are not always sent by interviewees, so this is another way for you to stand out from the crowd whether your interview went well or not.

A thank-you letter allows you to provide more information or reminders about your suitability for the position, as well as keep your name fresh in the interviewer's mind. However, consider sending a card instead of a letter. Why? Because a card will stand out in the pile of mail sitting on the interviewer's desk—just by virtue of the different size and shape of envelope—and therefore more likely to be opened quickly. You can even personalize a card further by finding something that appeals to the recipient, for instance, you note that she has several prints of jazz singers or a collection of giraffes—find a card that reflects the particular interest.

Dear Mr. Franks,

Thank you for taking the time to meet and discuss the marketing position at HerbCon with me. I really appreciate the time you spent acquainting me with your company and I'm even more convinced that my background and skills are a good match for your needs.

I look forward, Mr. Franks, to hearing from you concerning your hiring decision and once again, thank you for your time and consideration.

Sincerely,
Bob Daley

COACHES CORNER – VIII

Preparing Your Questions to Ask

AS YOU DO YOUR research in preparation for a potential interview, review the performance/ history of the company information. You want to be seen as an informed applicant able to answer questions or to explore further areas of the company AND you will be viewed as knowledgeable if you use this information to ask your own questions. There is always the possibility that you may not have received a detailed job description; your research will be valuable as you outline the job responsibility questions that you want answered.

Take the time to research relevant and insightful questions for each potential interviewer with whom you are scheduled to meet. Remember, in an interview session or a series of interviews, you will be meeting different interviewers responsible for giving you different information about the company and the position. Key here is that questions you might develop for HR will differ from those you prepare for a potential manager (also keep in mind that at this stage your questions should relate to organization and job description, NOT benefits).

Earlier in this book, we discussed how you may be asked to meet with your potential staff or peers—develop questions tailored to these audiences as well.

In a perfect world you should have the following information available and placed in your Briefing Book, before the interview day:

- the meeting schedule;
- names, titles/ positions of the people with whom you will meet; and
- times for each meeting.

Ideally, if you know you are a finalist for the position, you need to organize questions to ask your network contacts in order to reference check the company or confirm something you discovered. Better safe than sorry, right? Remember, it is an Art to be able to sell yourself during the interviewing process and at the same time be an investigative reporter in order to gather all the information to make a informed decision.

Generic Questions

The smart process is to review the generic questions and then design questions to reflect your research. For instance, by reviewing public finance reports, you discover that company's performance is ahead of last year's results, ask:

> *Do you think you can maintain your growth of 18%?*

or

> *Since you have the major market share tied up does the company plan to expand into new areas?*

Focused and Appropriate Questions

Key tip is until you get the offer and while you are still meeting/ interviewing with company personnel, all the questions you have considered will be about the job and the organization. Unless it is offered, don't go fishing for information about benefits or begin asking about your next career move in the company. There will be a time and place for those questions to be asked. If those areas don't develop naturally and you sense they are about to spring-board an offer on you, be prepared to ask questions (see examples below) or summarize if you have already been told:

- What are the core responsibilities of the position?
- Is the position new or a replacement? If new, why?
- What would you like done differently by the next person hired for this job?

More often than not, you will have performed in the position for which you are interviewing and should know from experience what worked and what didn't. Be prepared to explore areas of your responsibility that weren't supported previously. Make sure you have a clear idea of measurement.

- If we were sitting here a year from now having a conversation, how will we know that I have met or exceeded the job objections? How will I be measured?

This can also fit into determining if the position's objectives are realistic in your frame of reference. This also brings up the point: how is the objective to be funded?

- What are the strategic goals of this position and the time frame for them to be accomplished?
- Which goal is most pressing? What would you like to have done first or within the next two or three months?
- What level of authority will I have in determining methods of operation?
- What significant changes are being discussed that may not be evident to a new person?
- Where do you see the company heading in the next few years?
- How do you like your managers to communicate with you?
- What is the funding allocated for this position in relation to the goals? (should be asked later or only when appropriate)

If it seems like the interview may be ending and you still do not have a solid feeling about being a candidate, you may try this approach: ask,

Is there anything I discussed in my background that you may want me to explain further?

It's not asking for a decision, but it can clear up something that is on their mind that may not be positive.

Remember you can anticipate most situations
and questions. If you do your company research,
prepare and practice your responses you will
gain confidence and be successful.

COACHES CORNER - IX

Behaviors and Competencies

THE SELF-ANALYSIS OF WHAT you can do for a company is the foundation for conducting a successful job search campaign. The career/ job insights you'll gain can be organized into three broad categories: *what you know how to do, what you are willing to do,* and *how you will fit* (behavior) into the company's culture.

The resume which helped you get to an interview will display: your work history - *what you have done*; the accomplishments - *the will-do*; and the personal interview will handle *the fit*, which covers how compatible you are with the culture (style) and values of the company/ position. This preparation of work behaviors gives you advance knowledge of how to present your qualifications for the position.

The company will have their set of job behaviors to screen applicants. It goes without saying that learning as much as possible about the company, the position, the hiring authority, interviewers, and most importantly—the wants/ needs of the company, are essential.

In most interviewing situations you will have to prepare for the needs stated and those unstated, sometimes called by recruiters the "hidden agenda." Determining ahead of time how you might handle the surprise, unanticipated questions will help you to be more effective in the interview process— so you don't get flustered. In order to handle surprise questions, consider which accomplishments in your work experience might be used to answer a question or to make a point. The following information included with this Coaches Corner will provide you with a sound foundation:

    While you prepare to identify and group your behaviors as depicted in your accomplishments, note that the following broad areas will be measured as well as the specifics of the position for which you are interviewing.

Identity and Group Behaviors

    I.   Knowledge of the Industry

-what is your industry experience

-how did you secure the position you are occupying

    II.   Technical Knowledge

-not just I.T.

-how to do spreadsheets, Excel, Word, Lotus Notes, etc.

-your experience

    III.   Teamwork (behavior)

-working effectively with teams to accomplish organizational goals and anticipate and resolve problems;

-if in a management position, how did you build and manage the teams

    IV.   Decision-making (skills/ behavior)

-what steps do you follow

    V.   Ability to Transition to New Environments

-how well do you adjust to changes over which you have no control

-if some of you have been with an organization for a number of years (like 10-20 years), often you will be questioned as to your plans in making the transition

VI.   Performance

-going beyond the call of duty, managing for results

VII.   Personal Motivation (behavior)

-passion for what you do

VIII.   Initiative (behavior)

-do you have examples (list) of the ability to originate or follow through

IX.   Continuous Learning (behavior)

-as part of your working style, do you search for better ways; do you assimilate new job-related information

X.   Planning and Organizing (behavior)

-discuss management of resources, time management, setting priorities for subordinates

XI.   Communication (behavior)

-is your written as well as spoken communication to individuals and during group presentations effective?

-training?

-public representation?

XII.   Customer Service (skills)

-how adept are you with handling difficult situations, both internal and external?

XIII.   Empathy – Listening – Sensitivity (behavior)

-importance of feelings and needs of others?

In relationship building with your references, this list of behaviors can be a guide for you to refer to and often one/ two examples are discovered.

Performance Skills and Behaviors

Rapport Building	Planning/ Organizing
Work Ethics	Strategic Oriented
License/ Patent	Technical Knowledge
Risk-Taking	Materials Management
Training	Innovation - Creativity
Business Systems	Empathy/ Sensitivity
Quality Assurance	Participative Management
Self-Management	Problem Solving - Analysis
Energy	Organization/ planning
Customer Service	Continuous Learning
Decision Making	Detail – Coaching – Change
Goal Orientation	Investigative/ Fact-finding
Teamwork	Tenacity/ Flexibility

Conflict Management	Achievement oriented
Entrepreneurial	Leadership/ Influence
Safety - Health	Listening/ Diplomacy
Futuristic Thinking	Impact
Motivating	Delegation
Diplomacy	Persuasion
Financial/ Budget Ability	Presentation Group
Employment Development	Sales/ Marketing Oriented
Control – Process Oriented	Technical Requirements
Judgment	Communications - Oral
Innovation	Written Communications
Negotiation	Adaptability - Transition
Integrity	

COACHES CORNER X

The Other Side
What is the interviewer thinking about
during the interview?

THROUGHOUT OUR DISCUSSION the focus has been on you. You were asked to consider who you are in terms of behaviors. As a reminder, these are the individual traits, which you use to get work done, and to showcase who you are.

Next you were asked to consider what your job skills were and the depth of the skill(s), and knowledge.

We then suggested that this data would be used in discussions with a potential employer to showcase your FAB: *features*, *abilities* and *benefits*—bottom line: what you're bringing to the job. These are your job skill/ knowledge factors.

We also discussed how to use the SARB format: *situation*, *actions*, *results*, *behaviors*, as the structure to respond to all interview questions, including behavioral-based interviews. In fact, SARB can and should be used in any interview format as a way to get your winning message across.

One other important item in interview: it is absolutely critical that the question asked be listened to accurately—internalize the information. While the intent of some questions may be obvious—others may not, therefore you need to make a decision each time a question is asked, *what is the focus*?

Behavior, Definition, Possible Follow-up Question

So the logical question in your mind at this time is, how is my listener thinking about/ interpreting the information I have provided? To discuss, THE OTHER SIDE, we provide a layout of an actual interview. This layout will identify:

- the behavior;
- the definition; and,
- a possible question that may be asked.

Look closely at the definitions, as these are keys to effective answers. All of the behaviors were chosen because of their commonality to any job. The key will be to look at the definition and objective of the behavior and ask yourself the question: *What can I use from my background to showcase my effectiveness in this behavior?* Remember SARB.

In the real world, a company that uses a behavioral/ situational-based interview structure, will have identified the behaviors involved in a position; these are usually developed from the job description and management discussion. It is important to ask for a job description when getting ready for an interview (usually at the time of first contact with the company). You can trust your own instincts. You know, if you think about it, what success factors into your work; you also know who you are in terms of why people like you, so by all means, go out and sell these behaviors.

A caution:

It is not enough to memorize these behaviors and definitions, you will need to internalize them so that if the interviewer uses the terms in a different context you will be in tune with him or her. Remember the dance of the interviewer? Don't find yourself out of step!

Behavior	Definition	Possible Question
Adaptability	Being flexible and accommodating	Our atmosphere can be described as freewheeling and fast moving. Showcase for me how you would function in a fast moving operation.
Follow-up	The act of complying and making sure of desired results.	When working an assignment, give me an example of what you do to stay informed.
Teamwork	Banding together for common objectives	There is little doubt that working with others is key to success in any organization. Discuss a situation where you were able to influence a group to a desired outcome.
Customer Service	A buyer of products, services or client. Keep in mind that this could internal as well as external customers.	Discuss a situation in which you feel you contributed to the well-being of a customer.
Accountability	To be liable, answerable, responsible	Let's say you had a number of projects in the hopper of all varying degrees of importance, and one of import was not staying in line with the desired time lines. Discuss a time when this happened to you.

Critical thought:
You may not have had a situation that is being asked of you. In that case, it would be valuable for you to state what it is you do to avoid that kind of problem or what you would do if you had such a situation.

Behavior	Definition	Possible Question
Problem-solving	To decipher and find an answer	Tell me about a problem you faced; I would like to learn exactly how you go about dealing with a problem in its pieces.
Thinking	Using one's mind, reflecting, deliberate	Thinking about thinking is a difficult task; tell me how you go about identifying the key issues and the impact that they may have on your department.
Leadership	Working in the broadest sense in an organization and developing plans and influencing decisions which affect the organization's goals	Tell me about a decision you assisted others in making which had a profound impact on the organization or department.
Honesty	Integrity, honor, faithfulness principles	Discuss a situation in which you feel your integrity/ ethics were being tested.

Behavior	Definition	Possible Question
Composure	Self controlled, even-tempered, level-headedness	Discuss a situation, which would demonstrate your ability to stay focused during rapidly changing circumstances.
Versatility	Multi-faceted, resourceful, ingenious	Working with people can at times be a challenge, tell me about a time you assisted another person to become comfortable, one in which you had to modify your thinking to achieve the desired result.
Innovation	Departure from the old, introduction of new ideas, significant change	Describe a situation in which you presented a new thought, or a role you played in introducing a change to the organization or department.
Coaching	Being a mentor	Tell me about a challenging situation you have had with a problem employee by discussing what you did to turn the situation around and save the employee.

**It is a matter of getting the right words,
behaviors, into your answers.**

Behavior	Definition	Possible Question
Communication	The exchange of information and thoughts to influence a person or group	Tell me about a time when you had to rely on your communication skill to get something done.
Listening	To hear, to pay attention, to take notice, to internalize information	Being able to hear a message is very valuable in saving time; tell me about a time when your ability to pay attention really paid off for you.

You may be wondering how to answer the applicable questions. The key is to look at the definitions and then look at your SARBs; ask yourself: *How will I get the message across to the interviewer?*

It is a matter of getting the right words, behaviors, into your answers. Your SARBs are, in most cases, the answer. Ask yourself: *How well did I do with thinking through my work and thinking about myself?*

Coaches Corner XI

The Background Overview

THE BACKGROUND OVERVIEW was first mentioned in the reference chapter (Ch. 4) as an organizational tool. A careful and thorough completion of the *Background Overview* will begin to identify the groundwork for success in the development of your Career Roadmap. This process is all about doing first things first. In other words, if you are able to describe your ideal work environment or preferences coupled with what you do well and like to do, and then integrate your motivation, attitudes and job skills (MAS), most likely you will be able to build the roadmap or target specific jobs that progress to a career objective.

It is becoming clearer every day that the individuals who are going to be happy/ productive in their chosen professions in the future are taking ownership of their career—just as you are doing now. Once you have gathered background, interests, values, likes/ dislikes, and so on, look at your past work experiences in detail. Remember it takes time to think through and capture this information.

Knowing what you do well is essential for understanding your strengths and for linking your capabilities to specific occupations/ jobs/ careers. Also, you must connect your abilities and skills to a direction (roadmap) in identifying the right job or occupation. When you have defined your work values, interests, and preferences, you will have most of the necessary building blocks for setting your future goals and targeting your abilities toward specific jobs/ occupations.

General Information:

1.   What is the statement you use when asked *what do you do for a living*?

2.   Do you belong to any business or professional organizations that would be important to you in identifying what you like to be involved in or with?

3.   List any licenses or certifications.

4.   Any second language?

5.   Any additional training accomplished that you might explore for potential employment?

6.   What do you believe are your management assets/ behaviors? Projects; people; sales; budgets; product/ market awareness (list)?

7.   Are you able to describe:
     •your ideal job?
     •your ideal organization?

8.   Desired compensation?

9.   Would you relocate? Relocate later in your career?

10.   Are you willing to return to college or engage in additional career training?

11.   Were you part of any special task forces/ special committees?

12.   Often the intent behind the questions asked are: *why shouldn't we hire you* or *why should we hire you*? Think about this question and record what you would say.

Hint: the answer starts with: *If you do not need. . . .*

Or, if you were hiring yourself, tell why are you a good candidate. This question is somewhat premature to a specific occupation being determined, but there are behaviors that you still possess regardless of your future potential job.

13. What are some of your home-based interests: hobbies, building, campaigning, volunteering, home repair or decorating, art projects, or outside the home projects?

14. Work values are those things you like to do. They give pleasure and enjoyment. Most jobs (careers) involve a combination of likes and dislikes. By identifying what you both like and dislike about jobs, you should be able to determine a pattern. Complete the two exercises below to determine the work values most important to you—at present and in the future.

WORK VALUES:

1st   check only those that apply now;
2nd   circle the ones you would like to have in the future.

	Contribute to society		Be creative
	Contact with people		Supervise others
	Work alone		Work with details
	Work with a team		Gain recognition
	Compete with others		Acquire security
	Make decisions		Make a lot of money
	Work under pressure		Help others
	Solve problems		Acquire new knowledge
	Use power and authority		Take risks
	Self-employed		Work at own pace

Select the five work values from the previous exercise, which are *most* important to you and list them below.

Note: List any additional work values not listed above but are important to you.

Frustrations

15. In order to draw a complete roadmap, it is also necessary to note negatives. Develop a comprehensive list of your past and recent job frustrations and dissatisfactions. This will help identify negative factors to avoid in any potential occupations or future jobs.

 List, as well as rank in order, as many past and recent things that frustrated you or made you unhappy/ dissatisfied in your work.

Ranking

1.	
2.	
3.	
4.	
5.	
6.	
7.	
8.	
9.	

10.	
11.	
12.	

Achievements (SARB)

16. Lifetime achievements are a useful tool when clarifying your personal strengths and preferences. Past achievements often indicate talents, traits, abilities and skills, and may point to the future areas of occupation that you would consider.

Again what we want to visit are the achievements that may have been benchmarks for you or may have influenced your life. This list can be called successes. These are things you did/ do particularly well and of which you are proud.

Using the above descriptions as the bases of definition, what are your top ten achievements or successes? You may use work related or personal examples.

Here are some examples: introduced a new product; built a new home; started my own business; completed college; served as Chairperson of My Club, etc.

Write your responses on a separate piece of paper and describe why this event(s) is considered by you as important.

17. The things I enjoy most about work are

Why?

18. Characteristics of people I like working with:

Why?

Characteristics of people I do not enjoy working with:

Why?

19. Is there anything at this stage that you think is important to consider in building your career transition plan?

20. Is there anything or specific event you would do over in your life? in your work career? (of course, WHY is most important)

Career Analysis and Reflection

The next step in developing your Career Roadmap is a sentence completion exercise. The purpose is to analyze and reflect upon different aspects of your work career—this will assist you in goal-setting and targeting your abilities toward specific jobs. Remember that the important part of each answer will be to address the WHY!

1. I find that managing individuals/ functions is
2. The hardest part of managing is
3. My creative juices flow when
4. The hardest business decisions for me to make are
5. When someone gets in my way I

6. I am most productive when

7. I am least productive when

8. What makes me unique is

9. In business, politically I

10. My associates would describe me as

11. My clients (customers) think of me as

12. The major setback for me in my career was

13. When I think about doing something different I

14. The best thing about me is

15. What I like least about myself is

16. Security is
17. When confronted with a loss or disappointment I
18. The greatest lesson in life I have learned is
19. When I think back on my career I would
20. I truly believe my career options for the future are: a. b. c.

General feelings:

How do you feel now that that you have completed these questions/ this analysis? Describe:

To be successful in your objectives/ goals for your career plan, there are certain expectations you have in considering this event a success, what or how would you describe success in relation to this process? Why has this been a good or bad exercise for you?

If we were to happen to meet a year from now and were discussing your new career, what do you suppose we would be talking about? saying? What role would this text have played? What do you think might be different?

Note: This assessment is a very typical approach a career coach would take to help you in developing a career roadmap.

COACHES CORNER XII

Evaluating Job Offers

THE GOAL OF PROVIDING this working example is to equip you with a basic process to analyze and compare job offers. This format is one of many that you can use for evaluation. The key issue is to be prepared and employ a negotiation process that is a win-win for you and the potential employer.

Critical Junctures

Normally there are several critical junctures when probed or asked by a recruiter or interviewer about salary information. For the initial stages of the recruiting process (which usually occur over the phone) have a range researched and ready to deliver.

The next point is while interviewing with the company and they are trying to build a box that you fit into with salary issues, wants or desires.

The last juncture occurs if the applicant is inflexible or creative in the negotiation phase.

Once in awhile there is the applicant who receives an offer package that exceeds her expectations. We always suggest that there has to be an area or areas to discuss or apply some negotiating. Unless you are looking at a signed, sealed and now delivered hire package, remember you still are presenting yourself and being evaluated.

We have consulted on cases where the applicant lost a job over minor issues that, if left alone, could have been resolved after hiring. Many considerations are evaluated when establishing a starting salary for a recruited position. Usually the discussion begins with *what is your current salary level?*

If you are just graduating from college there may not be a salary history. To be prepared for the offer from the company recruiter, check with your campus career counselor—what are the competitive offers? If you can demonstrate some serious work responsibility while attending college you may get an offer in the higher percentile of the job grade.

What if you do not yet have a salary history?

Sell your behaviors—these are what you bring to the table as a recent graduate. More often than not the entry level positions are salaried the same and you get increases based upon your first year's performance. Best advice is to consider more than money as you begin or move up in your career. How are you going to be mentored into the mainstream of the company? Money always follows results.

Exact figures are important for your total compensation package. Do your homework; find market value on similar positions. You can use something like this for bonuses: *In the last five years my bonus has averaged X to X.* If you are pure salary use the average performance review increases (assuming there are some).

In today's world of work, benefits are very competitive and ever-changing. Depending on the position there may be other forms of compensation to discuss. If you are being pirated away from a company a big attraction is salary. When that is not the case you need to focus on results and knowledge you bring to the position so the company falls in love with you and money follows.

A Method to Evaluate Job Offers

The following information is only one way of many that you can use to evaluate job offers. The example following uses a numerical rating divided into four parts.

PART ONE:

Job Requirements

What is important to you? How much compromising will you have to do? It is important to first look at the job requirements.

If you are fortunate to have a job description, confirm that it is the latest version and the one followed. This is often overlooked in today's world of work due to downsizing, consolidations and mergers taking place. Organizations have not been able to keep up with the changes and re-do the job descriptions. On certain occasions the new hire will be responsible for pulling the functional aspects of the work into new descriptions/ responsibilities.

It is a good idea to review your earlier list of what you identified in the job as important for you (*Coaches Corner XI*). Compare this list to the job you have been offered to see if you have at least matched 80-90% of your wants. In an effort to help you with the thought process review the following factors:

- Job requirements
- Is there opportunity for growth
- Salary level—ideal or acceptable
- Is there any employment agreement possible
- Quality of life issues - Working conditions
- Relocation - Risk/ family impact/ twelve month move back agreement
- Benefits - What percentage paid by employee - effective date of coverage
- Vacation - (this is compensation too)
- Bonus - 401k match
- Stock options - profit sharing/ pension

Let's take a look at each factor and your considerations or compromises.
   1.   Job Requirements

   Key Considerations:

- Does my experience match or exceed what they are looking for?

- Am I excited about the opportunity?

- Will the job be challenging? Will I be proud to say I work for this company?

- Is there enough room for me to be myself? Any room for creativity?

- What are the chances for career advancement?

- Am I okay with the travel required?

- What is my manager's style of supervision? Will I have autonomy?

- Is it possible to work out of my home?

- What plans are there for continued education, training, and is there tuition refund?

- Are the goals for me reasonable? Are there ample resources/ budget/ P&L, what is my accountability here?

- Is there been discussion about my sponsorship into the company?

- What is the political environment like?

- What appears to be the amount of change that is involved or your read on the willingness to change?

- Why do I "feel" I want this job?

- How do my behaviors fit the management group?

> Compare your goals with your answers.
> Determine what your minimum level of acceptance will be for each key requirement.
> What is the deal breaking point?

2. Career Roadmap

Key considerations:

- Will the position offer the career path I want to follow?
- How are people promoted in this organization?
- Will there be training provided by the company?
- Do the goals that I have planned for myself match with the company's growth?

3. Salary Level –Financial

Key considerations:

- Does THE salary being offered meet my requirements?
- Consider the performance review: How will I be measured? What are my accountabilities in relationship to my goals?
- Do I have all the information necessary in regards to bonuses/ profit sharing/ fringe benefits/ relocation policy, if that happens to part of the deal?

4. Security

Key requirements:

- Are the financials healthy for the company?
- What are the plans for the future; how will that

affect me?

- Market share - product competition?
- What is the reputation of the company?
- What is the culture like?
- What is the reason given as to why my position is open?
- Is the company union or non-union?
- EEOC status - union grievances? Liquidations on-going?
- The 401k match. What is the average tenure? Pending mergers – consolidations - history of downsizings?

5. Quality of Life Issues - Working Conditions

Key Requirements:

- What is the turnover like? Any smiling faces?
- How were the attitudes of the people I met?
- Is there anything about my boss I didn't like? Will it get to me?
- What will my first 90 days be like? Will I be accepted quickly?
- What are the true working hours of my peer group? Is there potential conflict with my quality of life?

6. Relocation Now or In The Future

Key requirements:

- Is the geographical locale to my liking? Family acceptance?
- In the future, if I had to change jobs, would this locale be a good place to do that?
- Culture - Weather - Political Environment -

Taxes?

- Are there advanced education facilities? If you have children – what is the education quality in public schools? Special Ed? Private schools?
- Can my spouse find work?
- Location of corporate offices?
- What are the relocation monies like? Do I have to spend any of my own assets? Will the company let me wait a year before buying? Temporary housing, how long? Research the unfamiliar areas and look at the parameters. What if I didn't move? How much further ahead will I move my career objectives if I take this position?

7. Benefits – Vacation

Key requirements:

- Is the benefit package adequate? How much more or less is my contribution? How soon can I enroll? Will the company pay for any waiting period for benefits? Are there any special Executive Perks - (paid up term insurance). STD - LTD, Parent Care, etc.
- Vacation - Sick Days - Holidays?

Review and examine the areas of concern and if necessary weigh the importance to the final decision.

PART TWO:

Establishing Importance of Factors: Selected–Weighting

After you have reviewed the list of key job requirements, it is important to determine the level of importance for each factor relative to the others on your list. If you work through this process it will help with reducing the common, "everything is important" situation. Yes it is, but are there deal breakers? In today's world of work, some companies will not pay relocation or will only pay a set amount. Tough decisions!

By discussing these areas before the final job offer you are in a better informed position to know when and where (if necessary) to compromise or not. In trying to keep the values simple, we suggest just use a percentage weight and make sure it adds up to 100%.

Prioritizing the Requirements

Placing a value as to the importance of the requirements is the next step. We recommend you take the Job Requirements in the seven categories and apply a weight. Next you can take the priority items selected in each job requirement section and place a value on them.

Example:

Job requirements/ fit	25
Career roadmap	15
Salary level	20
Employment agreement	05
Quality of working conditions	05
Relocation	15
Benefits - vacation	05
Bonus - 401k	10

100%

We didn't use any specific approach in the selection of the priorities. Each person has his/her own set of priorities to evaluate. The exercise is designed to help you be better prepared to deal with the job offers so they are a smooth process and you are an informed buyer. If you have several job offers, you can use this system for comparison.

PART THREE:

Job Weighting

How does the job offer match with your preferred requirements? Now that you have determined the weight of the job factors important to you, establish to what degree each job offer fulfills the objectives of your factors.

Suggested criteria to use:

Five points	- exceeds my objective
Four	- market value, good
Three	- meets my minimum
Two	- falls short
One	- short fall, negotiation

PART FOUR:

Comparison of Jobs – Score

Added Value – Score

Summarize the information to develop the point value for each job. The purpose of this exercise is designed to give you a specific comparison and knowledge to maximize your discussions in the interviewing process. Again this is meant to be a tool for you. In the negotiation phase, you still have to be selling as you are negotiating. To know what to compromise on ahead of time is a powerful tool. You can do some dealing to get everything you can. You don't want to leave money on the discussion table.

May you SECURE many offers and LAND your dream job! Good Luck.

COACHES CORNER XIII

Likeability Factor

Likeability, what role does that play in the interview process? I thought all that was necessary during an interview was to match my job skills to the requirements of the open position. If I do that effectively, where does likeability come in and what is it anyway?

To discover the answers to the above questions it is important to consider the following: Many of the candidates likely have the same job skills as you, or they would not be a candidate for the position; what will make you stand out from other candidates? You may assume that your achievements will make the difference—stop there. Think about the other resumes the company has seen; they will also contain impressive achievements. You cannot count on these to help you stand out in an interview.

In his book, *The Likeability Factor: How to Boost Your Likeability Factor*, Tim Sanders defines it as a skill that reflects one's capacity to consistently produce the right emotions in the lives of people. He says this can be done by friendliness, relevance, empathy and realness. We would like to expand this thinking: Likeability is the ability to make someone aware of who we are, what we use to get work done — factor this thinking into our achievements — thus demonstrating how our values, beliefs, traits and habits have assured our success in the past and will do so in the future.

There is another very key role for the items that make up the likeability factor and that is fit to an organization and to a new boss. Fit is a cultural issue and it is one of the issues which must be explored during an interview. The importance of an all-round fit cannot be over-emphasized; without it, unpleasant working conditions will exist as well as unhappiness. The only way for you, as a job applicant, to develop a picture of the right cultural fit is to know your own behaviors, traits, values and habits. If you do not know them then you have nothing to measure against as you are researching prospective companies.

> Your likeability factor makes you to
> stand out from other candidates.

What follows in this section is a discussion of what to look at in identifying your likeability factor, based upon our experience with hundreds of hiring authorities. A key point that arises 100% of the time during a discussion of whether or not to extend a job offer to an applicant isn't about knowledge or skills: it is about how well the interviewers "liked" some aspect of the candidate's personal makeup.

While working on this project Dave and I have had a great many discussions involving interviews, those of the past and interviews of the present. Our experiences with interviewees, assessing interviewees, developing and making management presentations on potential candidates cover a combined 80 years of interviewing and hiring.

As we worked through our experiences and thoughts we seemed to be continually led to recognize how hiring authorities, individually and in groups, talked about the qualities of potential candidates. What always came to mind was that, as these discussions took place, it was not job skills and knowledge that were the focus but rather what the hiring authority LIKED about a potential candidate. That makes sense if you think about it a moment. Consider that by the time a potential candidate's paperwork gets into the final review process, the job's hard skills have already been verified—this is a person who has what is required and there is nothing more to talk about in that arena. So, what is left? The question of why, I, the hiring authority, would want to work with the person.

Now stop and think for a moment, how likely is it that someone is going to want to work with you because you know a particular financial structure, or a particular wage and salary system, or you know about P&Ls, or you are familiar with a particular IT system? Our guess is that you must conclude that there is more to working with someone than the hard skills they bring to the table. What is left? Go back to the previous discussion—the word *LIKE* should stand out to you.

Read any definition of *LIKE*, you will notice things like pleasing, agreeable, amiable, attitude, showing a genuine interest in others, ability to look people in the eye while talking, showing empathy, good listening skills—to put it into the language of this book: the ability to show what you are made up of in terms of personable behaviors. What you do not read is mention of any hard skills because, as we have said, you won't be considered likeable because you know how to run a computer. Bottom line is that as we talked about our experiences, it was easy for us to see that just about every one of the "to hire discussions" started with the statement, *I LIKE*.

Strength in hard skills does not equal likeability.

Several years ago we started coaching clients on the issue of how to develop their *LIKEABILITY FACTOR*. To do that we had to determine what kinds of on-the-job or personal skills would go into making up a person's likeability factor. What evolved with time and research, was recognition that getting work done was not due to a piece of job knowledge, but rather a personal trait. It was easy for us to transition to the thinking that a person's *LIKEABILITY FACTOR* is made up of such items as the ability to communicate, and the ability to listen. Creativity, comfort around managers or any authority figure, interpersonal savvy, political savvy, patience, perspective, negotiation, team work, decision-making process, versatility just to name a few (see Chapter 2 for a full list).

Research will show that about 65 competencies or behaviors exist. A requirement for you is to study and to apply each one to your achievements then determine what you feel you can demonstrate and sell to a prospective employer. Guess what? It is unlikely that you will find that all of the competencies are core strengths for you: we are not made up that way. Successful habits tend to repeat themselves and if you work at it, you will determine that you have about 15 to 18 behaviors, habits, traits, values, which are key in your life and that you use each day to get work done. These are your likeability factors!

Identify your key likeability factors
from the list of behaviors or competencies in chapter 2.

The next and very important question is: How do I determine who or what I am? As we suggested back in chapter 2, one way is to look at what you gained out of your formative years. Funny thing about these early experiences, they tend to stay with us; yes, they are modified, but the basic feelings, beliefs, traits and habits are still there and they represent the real you. These are the items that will assist in moving you into the *likeable* range during an interview. Another way is to get on the internet and begin to study competencies, and determine how various sources are talking about them.

As you begin to identify the qualities that represent you, the next step is to apply them to your work. It needs to be pointed out that teamwork, for instance, is not a stand-alone item, but is made up of many other behaviors. Consider for the moment that to be effective with a team, you must be a good communicator, listener, and have interaction skills; you need to be able to build rapport; you need to be perceptive, show empathy, know how to translate corporate goals into team goals, and be able to size up people. There could be others, however; when you select a personal strength, trait or habit that you plan to sell, you will need to know what goes into that particular behavior.

Knowing what comprised a distinguishing strength will give you the information to use when selling it during an interview. Do not forget SARB, that last letter stands for *behaviors* and this is where you will use your personal traits during an interview.

A recent survey of over 800 managers and hiring professionals concluded that 67% would hire an applicant with strong, "demonstrated" personal skills, traits, habits, but whose technical skills were lacking. Only 9% said they would hire someone who had strong technical skills but weak interpersonal skills. The study went on to suggest that technical skills were the easiest to talk about because they are what we do each day of our working lives. Think about it; how often do you take time, on the job or at home, to think about what you used in terms of traits and habits to get a project done? If you're like most folks, almost no time is taken for such thinking. However in the world of behavioral or competency-based interviewing it is a must in order to be successful. It is crucial that you know which traits, behaviors, or habits you use to get work done each day.

GLOSSARY
of Why Shouldn't We Hire You? Terms

Agency. a business or service authorized to act for others.

Accomplishments. clusters of job skills, abilities, knowledge used to successfully perform jobs.

Attitudes. beliefs, feelings, values, dispositions to act in certain ways; behaviors.

Briefing Book. an organized collection of reference materials about a target company; contains the research you have done on the company and maybe a copy of the company's home page or logo. This is the career roadmap.

CEO. Chief Executive Officer. The executive who is responsible for a company's operations.

CFO. Chief Financial Officer. The executive who is responsible for financial planning and record keeping of a company.

COO. Chief Operating Officer. The executive who is responsible for the day-to-day management of a company.

Competencies/ behaviors. specific behavioral traits and attitudes that an individual uses to get work done with and through people.

Cost of living averages. cost of living takes into account items from six broad categories: groceries, housing, transportation, utilities, health care and miscellaneous goods and services. Basically it tells you how much it costs to live in a certain area. There are a variety of cost of living calculators available on the Internet: type "cost of living calculator" into your search engine.

Chronology of Employment. where you were employed, the dates you worked there, company titles, and briefly, what tasks and responsibilities were required of you.

Culture. the values, beliefs, rules of conduct and other predominant attitudes and behaviors that characterize the functioning of a company or organization.

EEOC. US Equal Employment Opportunity Commission. Federal agency that oversees unfair employment practices.

Employment agreement terms. basics include: term, responsibility, compensation, benefits and severance.

FAB. acronym for: Features. Advantages. Benefits. A marketing term used here to describe you, the product: your features, the advantages you bring to a company and how you can benefit the company.

Gap analysis. a business concept, to study the difference between 2 states or ideas for the purpose of determining how to get from one to the other. In this book we refer to your own gap analysis where you research to find a company's needs and then match your strengths to their deficient areas.

HR. Human Resources. Individuals within a firm who are responsible for hiring, firing, training and other personnel issues.

Job responsibility negotiation. negotiations that involve the interviewee's skills in relation to the job description.

Job Search Board of Directors. friends, colleagues, contacts who agree to support you through the job search with advice, contacts, references and so on.

Knowledge. the result of perception, learning and reason. For example, intellectual property that someone has about their industry, their job function, the company, the history of the organization, the key players, the politics, and themselves.

Likeability factor. an individual getting his/ her personal attributes message across to another person: using behaviors to develop rapport and trust. Good initial presentation of self so the interviewer feels positive!

MAS. acronym for: Motivation, attitude and skills.

P/L. Profit/ loss

References. a person who can recommend or vouch for another person. Strong references can play a key role in securing a position.

Retained recruiter. retained consultants from a search firm who work on behalf of clients to fill jobs. It is wise to remember that recruiters do not work for you—they work for and are paid by their client, a company, and they have the company's best interests at heart.

SARB. acronym for: Situation, Action, Results, Behaviors. A method used to present information in an interview that is comprehensive, impactful and succinct.

Skills/ job knowledge. application of knowledge; an ability acquired by training and experience to provide a solution, expertise or competency.

Strength. an asset; a quality or characteristic that is valuable or useful. Behaviors are strengths.

Vignette. a comprehensive, organized, succinct description; in the interviewing context vignettes are organized using SARB in order to highlight past accomplishments that demonstrate job knowledge and competencies and how these will benefit or address problems of a company.

Recommended Resources
Mentioned in *Why Shouldn't We Hire You*?

Bolles, Richard. What *Color is Your Parachute*? Berkeley, California: Ten Speed Press, 2004.
- practical guide for job seekers and those looking to career transition

Canfield, Jack et al. *The Power of Focus: How to Hit Your Business, Personal and Financial Targets with Absolute Certainty.* Florida: Health Communications, Inc., 2002
- clear, simple, roadmap that shows you how to focus on what is important in your life as well as career

Enelow, Wendy S. 1500+ *Key Words for $100,000+ Jobs*. Virginia: Impact Publications, 1998.
- guide to the selection and use of keywords to build powerful resumes

Sanders, Tim. The Likeability Factor: How to Boost Your Likeability Factor and Achieve Your Life's Dreams. New York:Three Rivers Press, 2006
- shows you how you can measure and increase your likeability

Lucht, John.. *Rites of Passage: Your Insider's Lifetime Guide to Executive Job-Changing and Faster Career Progress in the 21st Century.* Revised and Updated Version. New York: The Viceroy Press, 2000.
- good reference for information about how to work with search firms

Tarrant, John with Paul Fargis. *Perks and Parachutes.* New York: Times Business, 1997.
- helpful book that deals with employment agreements, conditions of employment, contracts, options, deferred income and much more

Welch, Jack. *Jack: Straight From the Gut.* New York: Warner Business Books, 2003.
- autobiographical book from the CEO of GE

Wood, Lamont. *Your 24/7 Online Job Search Guide.* New York: John Wiley & Sons, Inc., 2002.
- assistance for those seeking job opportunities on line

Reference:

The Directory of Executive Recruiters. Peterborough, NH: Kennedy Information, 2005.
- connects job seekers and recruiters; updated yearly and also available on-line

Web Sites (including additional useful sites):

Website address	Description
www.bls.gov	-Occupational Outlook Handbook contains profiles of many careers and associated links for further info
www.careerbuilders.com	–online job search
www.careervoyages.gov/ careercompass-main.com	-enter your interests, and a list of suitable careers is generated
www.craiglist.org	-online job search
www.firstgove.gov/ AgenciesFederal/All_Agencies/ index.shtml	- gateway to 150+ federal agency sites
www.hoovers.com	– research companies, industries, business people
www.hotjobs.com	–online job search
www.Indeed.com	-aggregate job listing site

www.job-hunt.org	-have a career goal and looking for a job
www.khake.com	-focus on careers that don't require a college degree
www.mylifecoach.com	-online 25 minute assessment to match your interests with a list (annotated) of suitable careers
www.monster.com	–online job search
www.onestopcoach.org	-resume posting, job listings, wage and occupational trends
www.rileyguide.com/prepare. html	-career and occupational guides, employment and industry trends, self-assessment resources
www.salary.com	–includes job salary calculator, cost of living, benefits calculator
www.salaryexpert.com	-estimate salary for hundreds of occupations adjusted by zip code

www.salarysource.com	–tool for assessing current market value of over 350 benchmark positions
www.Simplyhired.com	-job listings from hundreds of employment websites
www.usajobs.gov	-listing of more than 20 000 federal job openings
www.wageweb.com	– online salary service that provides information on over 170 benchmark positions
finance.yahoo.com	-Yahoo! Financial
goliath.ecnext.com	-Gales Media Info –company profiles
ipl.si.umich.edu/div/subject /browse/ref09.00.00/	-portal links to online directories of professional association sites
online.wsj.com	-Wall Street Journal Online

INDEX